Contents

APPLE PIE BY GRANDMA OPLE

Servings: 8 | Prep: 30m | Cooks: 1h | Total: 1h30m

NUTRITION FACTS

Calories: 512 | Carbohydrates: 67.8g | Fat: 26.7g | Protein: 3.6g | Cholesterol: 31mg

INGREDIENTS

- 1 recipe pastry for a 9 inch double crust pie
- 1/2 cup white sugar
- 1/2 cup unsalted butter
- 1/2 cup packed brown sugar
- 3 tablespoons all-purpose flour
- 8 Granny Smith apples - peeled, cored and sliced
- 1/4 cup water

DIRECTIONS

1. Preheat oven to 425 degrees F (220 degrees C). Melt the butter in a saucepan. Stir in flour to form a paste. Add water, white sugar and brown sugar, and bring to a boil. Reduce temperature and let simmer.
2. Place the bottom crust in your pan. Fill with apples, mounded slightly. Cover with a lattice work crust. Gently pour the sugar and butter liquid over the crust. Pour slowly so that it does not run off.
3. Bake 15 minutes in the preheated oven. Reduce the temperature to 350 degrees F (175 degrees C). Continue baking for 35 to 45 minutes, until apples are soft.

BEST BROWNIES

Servings: 16 | Prep: 25m | Cooks: 35m | Total: 1h

NUTRITION FACTS

Calories: 183 | Carbohydrates: 25.7g | Fat: 9g | Protein: 1.8g | Cholesterol: 44mg

INGREDIENTS

- 1/2 cup butter
- 1/3 cup unsweetened cocoa powder
- 1 cup white sugar
- 1/2 cup all-purpose flour
- 2 eggs
- 1/4 teaspoon salt
- 1 teaspoon vanilla extract

- 1/4 teaspoon baking powder
- 3 tablespoons butter, softened
- 1 teaspoon vanilla extract
- 3 tablespoons unsweetened cocoa powder
- 1 cup confectioners' sugar
- 1 tablespoon honey

DIRECTIONS

1. Preheat oven to 350 degrees F (175 degrees C). Grease and flour an 8-inch square pan.
2. In a large saucepan, melt 1/2 cup butter. Remove from heat, and stir in sugar, eggs, and 1 teaspoon vanilla. Beat in 1/3 cup cocoa, 1/2 cup flour, salt, and baking powder. Spread batter into prepared pan.
3. Bake in preheated oven for 25 to 30 minutes. Do not overcook.
4. To Make Frosting: Combine 3 tablespoons softened butter, 3 tablespoons cocoa, honey, 1 teaspoon vanilla extract, and 1 cup confectioners' sugar. Stir until smooth. Frost brownies while they are still warm.

AWARD WINNING SOFT CHOCOLATE CHIP COOKIES
Servings: 72 | Prep: 15m | Cooks: 12m | Total: 1h40m

NUTRITION FACTS

Calories: 177 | Carbohydrates: 20.7g | Fat: 10.5g | Protein: 2.1g | Cholesterol: 24mg

INGREDIENTS

- 4 1/2 cups all-purpose flour
- 2 (3.4 ounce) packages instant vanilla pudding mix
- 2 teaspoons baking soda
- 4 eggs
- 2 cups butter, softened
- 2 teaspoons vanilla extract
- 1 1/2 cups packed brown sugar
- 4 cups semisweet chocolate chips
- 1/2 cup white sugar
- 2 cups chopped walnuts (optional)

DIRECTIONS

1. Preheat oven to 350 degrees F (175 degrees C). Sift together the flour and baking soda, set aside.

2. In a large bowl, cream together the butter, brown sugar, and white sugar. Beat in the instant pudding mix until blended. Stir in the eggs and vanilla. Blend in the flour mixture. Finally, stir in the chocolate chips and nuts. Drop cookies by rounded spoonfuls onto ungreased cookie sheets.

3. Bake for 10 to 12 minutes in the preheated oven. Edges should be golden brown.

APPLE CRISP

Servings: 12 | Prep: 30m | Cooks: 45m | Total: 1h20m

NUTRITION FACTS

Calories: 316 | Carbohydrates: 60.5g | Fat: 8.4g | Protein: 2.4g | Cholesterol: 20mg

INGREDIENTS

- 10 cups all-purpose apples, peeled, cored and sliced
- 1 cup all-purpose flour
- 1 cup white sugar
- 1 cup packed brown sugar
- 1 tablespoon all-purpose flour
- 1/4 teaspoon baking powder
- 1 teaspoon ground cinnamon
- 1/4 teaspoon baking soda
- 1/2 cup water
- 1/2 cup butter, melted
- 1 cup quick-cooking oats

DIRECTIONS

1. Preheat oven to 350 degrees F (175 degree C).
2. Place the sliced apples in a 9x13 inch pan. Mix the white sugar, 1 tablespoon flour and ground cinnamon together, and sprinkle over apples. Pour water evenly over all.
3. Combine the oats, 1 cup flour, brown sugar, baking powder, baking soda and melted butter together. Crumble evenly over the apple mixture.
4. Bake at 350 degrees F (175 degrees C) for about 45 minutes.

EASY SUGAR COOKIES

Servings: 48 | Prep: 15m | Cooks: 10m | Total: 25m

NUTRITION FACTS

Calories: 86 | Carbohydrates: 11.7g | Fat: 4g | Protein: 0.9g | Cholesterol: 14mg

INGREDIENTS

- 2 3/4 cups all-purpose flour
- 1 1/2 cups white sugar
- 1 teaspoon baking soda
- 1 egg
- 1/2 teaspoon baking powder
- 1 teaspoon vanilla extract
- 1 cup butter, softened

DIRECTIONS

1. Preheat oven to 375 degrees F (190 degrees C). In a small bowl, stir together flour, baking soda, and baking powder. Set aside.
2. In a large bowl, cream together the butter and sugar until smooth. Beat in egg and vanilla. Gradually blend in the dry ingredients. Roll rounded teaspoonfuls of dough into balls, and place onto ungreased cookie sheets.
3. Bake 8 to 10 minutes in the preheated oven, or until golden. Let stand on cookie sheet two minutes before removing to cool on wire racks.

CHANTAL'S NEW YORK CHEESECAKE

Servings: 12 | Prep: 30m | Cooks: 1h | Total: 7h30m | Additional: 6h

NUTRITION FACTS

Calories: 533 | Carbohydrates: 44.2g | Fat: 35.7g | Protein: 10.3g | Cholesterol: 159mg

INGREDIENTS

- 15 graham crackers, crushed
- 4 eggs
- 2 tablespoons butter, melted
- 1 cup sour cream
- 4 (8 ounce) packages cream cheese
- 1 tablespoon vanilla extract
- 1 1/2 cups white sugar
- 1/4 cup all-purpose flour
- 3/4 cup milk

DIRECTIONS

1. Preheat oven to 350 degrees F (175 degrees C). Grease a 9 inch springform pan.
2. In a medium bowl, mix graham cracker crumbs with melted butter. Press onto bottom of springform pan.

3. In a large bowl, mix cream cheese with sugar until smooth. Blend in milk, and then mix in the eggs one at a time, mixing just enough to incorporate. Mix in sour cream, vanilla and flour until smooth. Pour filling into prepared crust.

4. Bake in preheated oven for 1 hour. Turn the oven off, and let cake cool in oven with the door closed for 5 to 6 hours; this prevents cracking. Chill in refrigerator until serving.

CARROT CAKE

Servings: 18 | Prep: 1h | Cooks: 1h | Total: 2h | Additional: 30m

NUTRITION FACTS

Calories: 575 | Carbohydrates: 63.7g | Fat: 34.8g | Protein: 5.1g | Cholesterol: 69mg

INGREDIENTS

- 4 eggs
- 2 teaspoons ground cinnamon
- 1 1/4 vegetable oil
- 3 cups grated carrots
- 2 cups white sugar
- 1 cup chopped pecans
- 2 teaspoons vanilla extract
- 1/2 cup butter, softened
- 2 cups all-purpose flour
- 8 ounces cream cheese, softened
- 2 teaspoons baking soda
- 4 cups confectioners' sugar
- 2 teaspoons baking powder
- 1 teaspoon vanilla extract
- 1/2 teaspoon salt
- 1 cup chopped pecans

DIRECTIONS

1. Preheat oven to 350 degrees F (175 degrees C). Grease and flour a 9x13 inch pan.

2. In a large bowl, beat together eggs, oil, white sugar and 2 teaspoons vanilla. Mix in flour, baking soda, baking powder, salt and cinnamon. Stir in carrots. Fold in pecans. Pour into prepared pan.

3. Bake in the preheated oven for 40 to 50 minutes, or until a toothpick inserted into the center of the cake comes out clean. Let cool in pan for 10 minutes, then turn out onto a wire rack and cool completely.

4. To Make Frosting: In a medium bowl, combine butter, cream cheese, confectioners' sugar and 1 teaspoon vanilla. Beat until the mixture is smooth and creamy. Stir in chopped pecans. Frost the cooled cake.

CREAMY RICE PUDDING

Servings: 4 | Prep: 25m | Cooks: 20m | Total: 45m

NUTRITION FACTS

Calories: 366 | Carbohydrates: 67.6g | Fat: 6.9g | Protein: 8.8g | Cholesterol: 64mg

INGREDIENTS

- 3/4 cup uncooked white rice
- 1 egg, beaten
- 2 cups milk, divided
- 2/3 cup golden raisins
- 1/3 cup white sugar
- 1 tablespoon butter
- 1/4 teaspoon salt
- 1/2 teaspoon vanilla extract

DIRECTIONS

1. Bring 1 1/2 cups water to a boil in a saucepan; stir rice into boiling water. Reduce heat to low, cover, and simmer for 20 minutes.
2. In a clean saucepan, combine 1 1/2 cups cooked rice, 1 1/2 cups milk, sugar and salt. Cook over medium heat until thick and creamy, 15 to 20 minutes. Stir in remaining 1/2 cup milk, beaten egg, and raisins; cook 2 minutes more, stirring constantly. Remove from heat and stir in butter and vanilla.

BROOKE'S BEST BOMBSHELL BROWNIES

Servings: 24 | Prep: 15m | Cooks: 35m | Total: 50m

NUTRITION FACTS

Calories: 248 | Carbohydrates: 37.5g | Fat: 11.2g | Protein: 2.9g | Cholesterol: 51mg

INGREDIENTS

- 1 cup butter, melted
- 1 1/2 cups all-purpose flour
- 3 cups white sugar

- 1 cup unsweetened cocoa powder
- 1 tablespoon vanilla extract
- 1 teaspoon salt
- 4 eggs
- 1 cup semisweet chocolate chips

DIRECTIONS

1. Preheat oven to 350 degrees F (175 degrees C). Lightly grease a 9x13 baking dish.
2. Combine the melted butter, sugar, and vanilla in a large bowl. Beat in the eggs, one at a time, mixing well after each, until thoroughly blended.
3. Sift the flour, cocoa powder, and salt in a bowl. Gradually stir flour mixture into the egg mixture until blended. Stir in the chocolate morsels. Spread the batter evenly into the prepared baking dish.
4. Bake in preheated oven until an inserted toothpick comes out clean, 35 to 40 minutes. Remove, and cool pan on wire rack before cutting.

DOUBLE LAYER PUMPKIN CHEESECAKE

Servings: 8 | Prep: 30m | Cooks: 40m | Total: 4h10m | Additional: 3h

NUTRITION FACTS

Calories: 426 | Carbohydrates: 35.5g | Fat: 29g | Protein: 29g | Cholesterol: 108mg

INGREDIENTS

- 2 (8 ounce) packages cream cheese, softened
- 1/2 cup pumpkin puree
- 1/2 cup white sugar
- 1/2 teaspoon ground cinnamon
- 1/2 teaspoon vanilla extract
- 1 pinch ground cloves
- 2 eggs
- 1 pinch ground nutmeg
- 1 (9 inch) prepared graham cracker crust
- 1/2 cup frozen whipped topping, thawed

DIRECTIONS

1. Preheat oven to 325 degrees F (165 degrees C).
2. In a large bowl, combine cream cheese, sugar and vanilla. Beat until smooth. Blend in eggs one at a time. Remove 1 cup of batter and spread into bottom of crust; set aside.

3. Add pumpkin, cinnamon, cloves and nutmeg to the remaining batter and stir gently until well blended. Carefully spread over the batter in the crust.
4. Bake in preheated oven for 35 to 40 minutes, or until center is almost set. Allow to cool, then refrigerate for 3 hours or overnight. Cover with whipped topping before serving.

SIMPLE WHITE CAKE

Servings: 12 | Prep: 20m | Cooks: 30m | Total: 50m

NUTRITION FACTS

Calories: 209 | Carbohydrates: 29.4g | Fat: 8.9g | Protein: 3.1g | Cholesterol: 52mg

INGREDIENTS

- 1 cup white sugar
- 1 1/2 cups all-purpose flour
- 1/2 cup butter
- 1 3/4 teaspoons baking powder
- 2 eggs
- 1/2 cup milk
- 2 teaspoons vanilla extract

DIRECTIONS

1. Preheat oven to 350 degrees F (175 degrees C). Grease and flour a 9x9 inch pan or line a muffin pan with paper liners.
2. In a medium bowl, cream together the sugar and butter. Beat in the eggs, one at a time, then stir in the vanilla. Combine flour and baking powder, add to the creamed mixture and mix well. Finally stir in the milk until batter is smooth. Pour or spoon batter into the prepared pan.
3. Bake for 30 to 40 minutes in the preheated oven. For cupcakes, bake 20 to 25 minutes. Cake is done when it springs back to the touch.

BREAD PUDDING

Servings: 12 | Prep: 30m | Cooks: 45m | Total: 1h15m

NUTRITION FACTS

Calories: 165 | Carbohydrates: 26.5g | Fat: 4.8g | Protein: 4.6g | Cholesterol: 70mg

INGREDIENTS

- 6 slices day-old bread

- 2 cups milk
- 2 tablespoons butter, melted
- 3/4 cup white sugar
- 1/2 cup raisins (optional)
- 1 teaspoon ground cinnamon
- 4 eggs, beaten
- 1 teaspoon vanilla extract

DIRECTIONS

1. Preheat oven to 350 degrees F (175 degrees C).
2. Break bread into small pieces into an 8 inch square baking pan. Drizzle melted butter or margarine over bread. If desired, sprinkle with raisins.
3. In a medium mixing bowl, combine eggs, milk, sugar, cinnamon, and vanilla. Beat until well mixed. Pour over bread, and lightly push down with a fork until bread is covered and soaking up the egg mixture.
4. Bake in the preheated oven for 45 minutes, or until the top springs back when lightly tapped.

FRESH SOUTHERN PEACH COBBLER

Servings: 4 | Prep: 20m | Cooks: 40m | Total: 1h

NUTRITION FACTS

Calories: 562 | Carbohydrates: 99.4g | Fat: 17.g | Protein: 3.5g | Cholesterol: 46mg

INGREDIENTS

- 8 fresh peaches - peeled, pitted and sliced into thin wedges
- 1/4 cup white sugar
- 1/4 cup white sugar
- 1/4 cup brown sugar
- 1/4 cup brown sugar
- 1 teaspoon baking powder
- 1/4 teaspoon ground cinnamon
- 1/2 teaspoon salt
- 1/8 teaspoon ground nutmeg
- 6 tablespoons unsalted butter, chilled and cut into small pieces
- 1 teaspoon fresh lemon juice
- 1/4 cup boiling water
- 2 teaspoons cornstarch
- 3 tablespoons white sugar
- 1 cup all-purpose flour
- 1 teaspoon ground cinnamon

DIRECTIONS

1. Preheat oven to 425 degrees F (220 degrees C).
2. In a large bowl, combine peaches, 1/4 cup white sugar, 1/4 cup brown sugar, 1/4 teaspoon cinnamon, nutmeg, lemon juice, and cornstarch. Toss to coat evenly, and pour into a 2 quart baking dish. Bake in preheated oven for 10 minutes.
3. Meanwhile, in a large bowl, combine flour, 1/4 cup white sugar, 1/4 cup brown sugar, baking powder, and salt. Blend in butter with your fingertips, or a pastry blender, until mixture resembles coarse meal. Stir in water until just combined.
4. Remove peaches from oven, and drop spoonfuls of topping over them. Sprinkle entire cobbler with the sugar and cinnamon mixture. Bake until topping is golden, about 30 minutes.

BANANA PUDDING

Servings: 12 | Prep: 30m | Cooks: 3h | Total: 3h30m

NUTRITION FACTS

Calories: 398 | Carbohydrates: 55.1g | Fat: 16.6g | Protein: 7g | Cholesterol: 37mg

INGREDIENTS

- 1 (8 ounce) package cream cheese
- 1 teaspoon vanilla extract
- 1 (14 ounce) can sweetened condensed milk
- 1 (8 ounce) container frozen whipped topping, thawed
- 1 (5 ounce) package instant vanilla pudding mix
- 4 bananas, sliced
- 3 cups cold milk
- 1/2 (12 ounce) package vanilla wafers

DIRECTIONS

1. In a large bowl, beat cream cheese until fluffy. Beat in condensed milk, pudding mix, cold milk and vanilla until smooth. Fold in 1/2 of the whipped topping.
2. Line the bottom of a 9x13 inch dish with vanilla wafers. Arrange sliced bananas evenly over wafers. Spread with pudding mixture. Top with remaining whipped topping. Chill.

PERFECT PUMPKIN PIE

Servings: 8 | Prep: 15m | Cooks: 55m | Total: 1h10m

NUTRITION FACTS

Calories: 379 | Carbohydrates: 30.5g | Fat: 14.3g | Protein: 5.9g | Cholesterol: 64mg

INGREDIENTS

- 1 (15 ounce) can pumpkin
- 1/2 teaspoon ground ginger
- 1 (14 ounce) can EAGLE BRAND Sweetened Condensed Milk
- 1/2 teaspoon ground nutmeg
- 2 large eggs
- 1/2 teaspoon salt
- 1 teaspoon ground cinnamon
- 1 (9 inch) unbaked pie crust

DIRECTIONS

1. Preheat oven to 425 degrees F. Whisk pumpkin, sweetened condensed milk, eggs, spices and salt in medium bowl until smooth. Pour into crust. Bake 15 minutes.
2. Reduce oven temperature to 350 degrees F and continue baking 35 to 40 minutes or until knife inserted 1 inch from crust comes out clean. Cool. Garnish as desired. Store leftovers covered in refrigerator.

THE BEST LEMON BARS

Servings: 36| Prep: 15m | Cooks: 40m | Total: 55m

NUTRITION FACTS

Calories: 126 | Carbohydrates: 17.8g | Fat: 5.8g | Protein: 1.6g | Cholesterol: 34mg

INGREDIENTS

- 1 cup butter, softened
- 1 1/2 cups white sugar
- 1/2 cup white sugar
- 1/4 cup all-purpose flour
- 2 cups all-purpose flour
- 2 lemons, juiced
- 4 eggs

DIRECTIONS

1. Preheat oven to 350 degrees F (175 degrees C).
2. In a medium bowl, blend together softened butter, 2 cups flour and 1/2 cup sugar. Press into the bottom of an ungreased 9x13 inch pan.

3. Bake for 15 to 20 minutes in the preheated oven, or until firm and golden. In another bowl, whisk together the remaining 1 1/2 cups sugar and 1/4 cup flour. Whisk in the eggs and lemon juice. Pour over the baked crust.

4. Bake for an additional 20 minutes in the preheated oven. The bars will firm up as they cool. For a festive tray, make another pan using limes instead of lemons and adding a drop of green food coloring to give a very pale green. After both pans have cooled, cut into uniform 2 inch squares and arrange in a checker board fashion.

COUNTRY APPLE DUMPLINGS

Servings: 16 | Prep: 20m | Cooks: 45m | Total: 1h5m

NUTRITION FACTS

Calories: 333 | Carbohydrates: 38.5g | Fat: 19g | Protein: 2.7g | Cholesterol: 31mg

INGREDIENTS

- 2 large Granny Smith apples, peeled and cored
- 1 1/2 cups white sugar
- 2 (10 ounce) cans refrigerated crescent roll dough
- 1 teaspoon ground cinnamon
- 1 cup butter
- 1 (12 fluid ounce) can or bottle Mountain Dew

DIRECTIONS

1. Preheat the oven to 350 degrees F (175 degrees C). Grease a 9x13 inch baking dish.
2. Cut each apple into 8 wedges and set aside. Separate the crescent roll dough into triangles. Roll each apple wedge in crescent roll dough starting at the smallest end. Pinch to seal and place in the baking dish.
3. Melt butter in a small saucepan and stir in the sugar and cinnamon. Pour over the apple dumplings. Pour Mountain Dew(TM) over the dumplings.
4. Bake for 35 to 45 minutes in the preheated oven, or until golden brown.

SWEET POTATO PIE

Servings: 8 | Prep: 30m | Cooks: 1h50m | Total: 2h20m

NUTRITION FACTS

Calories: 389 | Carbohydrates: 47.8g | Fat: 20.6g | Protein: 4.5g | Cholesterol: 7mg

INGREDIENTS

- 1 (1 pound) sweet potato

- 1/2 teaspoon ground nutmeg
- 1/2 cup butter, softened
- 1/2 teaspoon ground cinnamon
- 1 cup white sugar
- 1 teaspoon vanilla extract
- 1/2 cup milk
- 1 (9 inch) unbaked pie crust
- 2 eggs

DIRECTIONS

1. Boil sweet potato whole in skin for 40 to 50 minutes, or until done. Run cold water over the sweet potato, and remove the skin.
2. Break apart sweet potato in a bowl. Add butter, and mix well with mixer. Stir in sugar, milk, eggs, nutmeg, cinnamon and vanilla. Beat on medium speed until mixture is smooth. Pour filling into an unbaked pie crust.
3. Bake at 350 degrees F (175 degrees C) for 55 to 60 minutes, or until knife inserted in center comes out clean. Pie will puff up like a souffle, and then will sink down as it cools.

EXTREME CHOCOLATE CAKE

Servings: 12 | Prep: 30m | Cooks: 35m | Total: 1h5m

NUTRITION FACTS

Calories: 655 | Carbohydrates: 111.1g | Fat: 24.6g | Protein: 7.3g | Cholesterol: 64mg

INGREDIENTS

- 2 cups white sugar
- 1/2 cup vegetable oil
- 1 3/4 cups all-purpose flour
- 2 teaspoons vanilla extract
- 3/4 cup unsweetened cocoa powder
- 1 cup boiling water
- 1 1/2 teaspoons baking soda
- 3/4 cup butter
- 1 1/2 teaspoons baking powder
- 1 1/2 cups unsweetened cocoa powder
- 1 teaspoon salt
- 5 1/3 cups confectioners' sugar
- 2 eggs
- 2/3 cup milk

- 1 cup milk
- 1 teaspoon vanilla extract

DIRECTIONS

1. Preheat oven to 350 degrees F (175 degrees C). Grease and flour two 9 inch cake pans.
2. Use the first set of ingredients to make the cake. In a medium bowl, stir together the sugar, flour, cocoa, baking soda, baking powder and salt. Add the eggs, milk, oil and vanilla, mix for 3 minutes with an electric mixer. Stir in the boiling water by hand. Pour evenly into the two prepared pans.
3. Bake for 30 to 35 minutes in the preheated oven, until a toothpick inserted comes out clean. Cool for 10 minutes before removing from pans to cool completely.
4. To make the frosting, use the second set of ingredients. Cream butter until light and fluffy. Stir in the cocoa and confectioners' sugar alternately with the milk and vanilla. Beat to a spreading consistency.
5. Split the layers of cooled cake horizontally, cover the top of each layer with frosting, then stack them onto a serving plate. Frost the outside of the cake.

ZUCCHINI BROWNIES

Servings: 24 | Prep: 15m | Cooks: 30m | Total: 45m

NUTRITION FACTS

Calories: 209 | Carbohydrates: 32.9g | Fat: 8.6g | Protein: 2.3g | Cholesterol: 0mg

INGREDIENTS

- 1/2 cup vegetable oil
- 2 cups shredded zucchini
- 1 1/2 cups white sugar
- 1/2 cup chopped walnuts
- 2 teaspoons vanilla extract
- 6 tablespoons unsweetened cocoa powder
- 2 cups all-purpose flour
- 1/4 cup margarine
- 1/2 cup unsweetened cocoa powder
- 2 cups confectioners' sugar
- 1 1/2 teaspoons baking soda
- 1/4 cup milk
- 1 teaspoon salt
- 1/2 teaspoon vanilla extract

DIRECTIONS

1. Preheat oven to 350 degrees F (175 degrees C). Grease and flour a 9x13 inch baking pan.
2. In a large bowl, mix together the oil, sugar and 2 teaspoons vanilla until well blended. Combine the flour, 1/2 cup cocoa, baking soda and salt; stir into the sugar mixture. Fold in the zucchini and walnuts. Spread evenly into the prepared pan.
3. Bake for 25 to 30 minutes in the preheated oven, until brownies spring back when gently touched.
4. Make frosting while brownies cool. Melt together the 6 tablespoons of cocoa and margarine; set aside to cool.
5. Meanwhile, blend together the confectioners' sugar, milk and 1/2 teaspoon vanilla. Stir in the cocoa mixture. Spread over cooled brownies before cutting into squares.

PEANUT BUTTER BARS

Servings: 12 | Prep: 25m | Cooks: 1h | Total: 1h25m | Additional: 1h

NUTRITION FACTS

Calories: 532 | Carbohydrates: 49.2g | Fat: 36.6g | Protein: 8.8g | Cholesterol: 41mg

INGREDIENTS

- 1 cup butter or margarine, melted
- 1 cup peanut butter
- 2 cups graham cracker crumbs
- 1 1/2 cups semisweet chocolate chips
- 2 cups confectioners' sugar
- 4 tablespoons peanut butter

DIRECTIONS

1. In a medium bowl, mix together the butter or margarine, graham cracker crumbs, confectioners' sugar, and 1 cup peanut butter until well blended. Press evenly into the bottom of an ungreased 9x13 inch pan.
2. In a metal bowl over simmering water, or in the microwave, melt the chocolate chips with the 4 tablespoons peanut butter, stirring occasionally until smooth. Spread over the prepared crust. Refrigerate for at least one hour before cutting into squares.

LEMON MERINGUE PIE

Servings: 8 | Prep: 30m | Cooks: 10m | Total: 40m

NUTRITION FACTS

Calories: 298 | Carbohydrates: 49.7g | Fat: 10.3g | Protein: 4.4g | Cholesterol: 110mg

INGREDIENTS

- 1 cup white sugar
- 2 tablespoons butter
- 2 tablespoons all-purpose flour
- 4 egg yolks, beaten
- 3 tablespoons cornstarch
- 1 (9 inch) pie crust, baked
- 1/4 teaspoon salt
- 4 egg whites
- 1 1/2 cups water
- 6 tablespoons white sugar
- 2 lemons, juiced and zested

DIRECTIONS

1. Preheat oven to 350 degrees F (175 degrees C).
2. To Make Lemon Filling: In a medium saucepan, whisk together 1 cup sugar, flour, cornstarch, and salt. Stir in water, lemon juice and lemon zest. Cook over medium-high heat, stirring frequently, until mixture comes to a boil. Stir in butter. Place egg yolks in a small bowl and gradually whisk in 1/2 cup of hot sugar mixture. Whisk egg yolk mixture back into remaining sugar mixture. Bring to a boil and continue to cook while stirring constantly until thick. Remove from heat. Pour filling into baked pastry shell.
3. To Make Meringue: In a large glass or metal bowl, whip egg whites until foamy. Add sugar gradually, and continue to whip until stiff peaks form. Spread meringue over pie, sealing the edges at the crust.
4. Bake in preheated oven for 10 minutes, or until meringue is golden brown.

OUTRAGEOUS CHOCOLATE CHIP COOKIES
Servings: 18 | Prep: 15m | Cooks: 10m | Total: 25m

NUTRITION FACTS

Calories: 207 | Carbohydrates: 23.7g | Fat: 12g | Protein: 3.6g | Cholesterol: 0mg

INGREDIENTS

- 1/2 cup butter
- 1 cup all-purpose flour
- 1/2 cup white sugar
- 1 teaspoon baking soda
- 1/3 cup packed brown sugar

- 1/4 teaspoon salt
- 1/2 cup peanut butter
- 1/2 cup rolled oats
- 1/2 teaspoon vanilla extract
- 1 cup semisweet chocolate chips
- 1 egg

DIRECTIONS

1. Preheat oven to 350 degrees F (175 degrees C).
2. In a medium bowl, cream together the butter, white sugar and brown sugar until smooth. Stir in the peanut butter, vanilla and egg until well blended. Combine the flour, baking soda and salt; stir into the batter just until moistened. Mix in the oats and chocolate chips until evenly distributed. Drop by tablespoonfuls on to lightly greased cookie sheets.
3. Bake for 10 to 12 minutes in the preheated oven, until the edges start to brown. Cool on cookie sheets for about 5 minutes before transferring to wire racks to cool completely.

BANANA CAKE

Servings: 18 | Prep: 30m | Cooks: 1h | Total: 2h30m | Additional: 1h

NUTRITION FACTS

Calories: 453 | Carbohydrates: 68.6g | Fat: 18.4g | Protein: 5.2g | Cholesterol: 79mg

INGREDIENTS

- 3/4 cup butter
- 1 1/2 cups buttermilk
- 2 1/8 cups white sugar
- 2 teaspoons lemon juice
- 3 eggs
- 1 1/2 cups mashed bananas
- 2 teaspoons vanilla extract
- 1/2 cup butter, softened
- 3 cups all-purpose flour
- 1 (8 ounce) package cream cheese, softened
- 1 1/2 teaspoons baking soda
- 3 1/2 cups confectioners' sugar
- 1/4 teaspoon salt
- 1 teaspoon vanilla extract

DIRECTIONS

1. Preheat oven to 275 degrees F (135 degrees C). Grease and flour a 9x13 inch pan. In a small bowl, mix mashed bananas with lemon juice, set aside. In a medium bowl, mix flour, baking soda and salt. Set aside.

2. In a large bowl, cream 3/4 cup butter and 2 1/8 cups sugar until light and fluffy. Beat in the eggs one at a time, then stir in 2 teaspoons vanilla. Beat in the flour mixture alternately with the buttermilk. Stir in banana mixture. Pour batter into prepared pan.

3. Bake in preheated oven for 1 hour, or until a toothpick inserted into the center of the cake comes out clean. Remove from oven and place directly into freezer for 45 minutes. This will make the cake very moist.

4. For the frosting: In a large bowl, cream 1/2 cup butter and cream cheese until smooth. Beat in 1 teaspoon vanilla. Add confectioners sugar and beat on low speed until combined, then on high until frosting is smooth. Spread on cooled cake.

SOPAPILLA CHEESECAKE PIE

Servings: 12 | Prep: 15m | Cooks: 45m | Total: 3h | Additional: 2h

NUTRITION FACTS

Calories: 481 | Carbohydrates: 50.8g | Fat: 28.7g | Protein: 5.6g | Cholesterol: 61mg

INGREDIENTS

- 2 (8 ounce) packages cream cheese, softened
- 1 teaspoon ground cinnamon
- 1 3/4 cups white sugar, divided
- 1/2 cup butter, room temperature
- 1 teaspoon Mexican vanilla extract
- 1/4 cup honey
- 2 (8 ounce) cans refrigerated crescent rolls

DIRECTIONS

1. Preheat an oven to 350 degrees F (175 degrees C). Prepare a 9x13 inch baking dish with cooking spray.

2. Beat the cream cheese with 1 cup of sugar and the vanilla extract in a bowl until smooth.

3. Unroll the cans of crescent roll dough, and use a rolling pin to shape each piece into 9x13 inch rectangles. Press one piece into the bottom of a 9x13 inch baking dish. Evenly spread the cream cheese mixture into the baking dish, then cover with the remaining piece of crescent dough. Stir together 3/4 cup of sugar, cinnamon, and butter. Dot the mixture over the top of the cheesecake.

4. Bake in the preheated oven until the crescent dough has puffed and turned golden brown, about 30 minutes. Remove from the oven and drizzle with honey. Cool completely in the pan before cutting into 12 squares.

AUNT TEEN'S CREAMY CHOCOLATE FUDGE
Servings: 48 | Prep: 10m | Cooks: 20m | Total: 30m

NUTRITION FACTS

Calories: 124 | Carbohydrates: 18.2g | Fat: 5.5g | Protein: 1.4g | Cholesterol: 5mg

INGREDIENTS

- 1 (7 ounce) jar marshmallow creme
- 2 cups milk chocolate chips
- 1 1/2 cups white sugar
- 1 cup semisweet chocolate chips
- 2/3 cup evaporated milk
- 1/2 cup chopped nuts
- 1/4 cup butter
- 1 teaspoon vanilla extract
- 1/4 teaspoon salt

DIRECTIONS

1. Line an 8x8 inch pan with aluminum foil. Set aside.
2. In a large saucepan over medium heat, combine marshmallow cream, sugar, evaporated milk, butter and salt. Bring to a full boil, and cook for 5 minutes, stirring constantly.
3. Remove from heat and pour in semisweet chocolate chips and milk chocolate chips. Stir until chocolate is melted and mixture is smooth. Stir in nuts and vanilla. Pour into prepared pan. Chill in refrigerator for 2 hours, or until firm.

EASIEST PEANUT BUTTER FUDGE
Servings: 15 | Prep: 15m | Cooks: 5m | Total: 1h20m

NUTRITION FACTS

Calories: 357 | Carbohydrates: 60.1g | Fat: 12.8g | Protein: 3.6g | Cholesterol: 17mg

INGREDIENTS

- 1/2 cup butter
- 3/4 cup peanut butter

- 1 (16 ounce) package brown sugar
- 1 teaspoon vanilla extract
- 1/2 cup milk
- 3 1/2 cups confectioners' sugar

DIRECTIONS

1. Melt butter in a medium saucepan over medium heat. Stir in brown sugar and milk. Bring to a boil and boil for 2 minutes, stirring frequently. Remove from heat. Stir in peanut butter and vanilla. Pour over confectioners' sugar in a large mixing bowl. Beat until smooth; pour into an 8x8 inch dish. Chill until firm and cut into squares.

NO BAKE COOKIES

Servings: 24 | Prep: 15m | Cooks: 25m | Total: 40m | Additional: 10m

NUTRITION FACTS

Calories: 172 | Carbohydrates: 25.2g | Fat: 7.3g | Protein: 3g | Cholesterol: 0mg

INGREDIENTS

- 2 cups white sugar
- 1 pinch salt
- 3 tablespoons unsweetened cocoa powder
- 3 cups quick cooking oats
- 1/2 cup margarine
- 1/2 cup peanut butter
- 1/2 cup milk
- 1 teaspoon vanilla extract

DIRECTIONS

1. In a saucepan bring sugar, cocoa, margarine, milk, and salt to a rapid boil for 1 minute.
2. Add quick cooking oats, peanut butter, and vanilla; mix well.
3. Working quickly, drop by teaspoonfuls onto waxed paper, and let cool.

CARAMEL POPCORN

Servings: 20 | Prep: 30m | Cooks: 1h | Total: 1h30m

NUTRITION FACTS

Calories: 253 | Carbohydrates: 32.8g | Fat: 14g | Protein: 0.9g | Cholesterol: 24mg

INGREDIENTS

- 1 cup butter
- 1/2 teaspoon baking soda
- 2 cups brown sugar
- 1 teaspoon vanilla extract
- 1/2 cup corn syrup
- 5 quarts popped popcorn
- 1 teaspoon salt

DIRECTIONS

1. Preheat oven to 250 degrees F (95 degrees C). Place popcorn in a very large bowl.
2. In a medium saucepan over medium heat, melt butter. Stir in brown sugar, corn syrup and salt. Bring to a boil, stirring constantly. Boil without stirring 4 minutes. Remove from heat and stir in soda and vanilla. Pour in a thin stream over popcorn, stirring to coat.
3. Place in two large shallow baking dishes and bake in preheated oven, stirring every 15 minutes, for 1 hour. Remove from oven and let cool completely before breaking into pieces.

NO BAKE PEANUT BUTTER PIE

Servings: 16 | Prep: 20m | Cooks: 2h | Total: 2h20m | Additional: 2h

NUTRITION FACTS

Calories: 432 | Carbohydrates: 41.4g | Fat: 27.8g | Protein: 7.2g | Cholesterol: 17mg

INGREDIENTS

- 1 (8 ounce) package cream cheese
- 1 cup milk
- 1 1/2 cups confectioners' sugar
- 1 (16 ounce) package frozen whipped topping, thawed
- 1 cup peanut butter
- 2 (9 inch) prepared graham cracker crusts

DIRECTIONS

1. Beat together cream cheese and confectioners' sugar. Mix in peanut butter and milk. Beat until smooth. Fold in whipped topping.
2. Spoon into two 9 inch graham cracker pie shells; cover, and freeze until firm.

CHOCOLATE TRIFLE

Servings: 12 | Prep: 30m | Cooks: 25m | Total: 8h55m

NUTRITION FACTS

Calories: 488 | Carbohydrates: 73.7g | Fat: 18.8g | Protein: 4.8g | Cholesterol: 12mg

INGREDIENTS

- 1 (19.8 ounce) package brownie mix
- 1 (8 ounce) container frozen whipped topping, thawed
- 1 (3.9 ounce) package instant chocolate pudding mix
- 1 (12 ounce) container frozen whipped topping, thawed
- 1/2 cup water
- 1 (1.5 ounce) bar chocolate candy
- 1 (14 ounce) can sweetened condensed milk

DIRECTIONS

1. Prepare brownie mix according to package directions and cool completely. Cut into 1 inch squares.
2. In a large bowl, combine pudding mix, water and sweetened condensed milk. Mix until smooth, then fold in 8 ounces whipped topping until no streaks remain.
3. In a trifle bowl or glass serving dish, place half of the brownies, half of the pudding mixture and half of the 12 ounce container of whipped topping. Repeat layers. Shave chocolate onto top layer for garnish. Refrigerate 8 hours before serving.

TIRAMISU

Servings: 12 | Prep: 35m | Cooks: 10m | Total: 5h | Additional: 4h15

NUTRITION FACTS

Calories: 387 | Carbohydrates: 22.7g | Fat: 30.5g | Protein: 6.6g | Cholesterol: 216mg

INGREDIENTS

- 6 egg yolks
- 1 pound mascarpone cheese
- 3/4 cup white sugar
- 1/4 cup strong brewed coffee, room temperature
- 2/3 cup milk
- 2 tablespoons rum
- 1 1/4 cups heavy cream
- 2 (3 ounce) packages ladyfinger cookies
- 1/2 teaspoon vanilla extract
- 1 tablespoon unsweetened cocoa powder

DIRECTIONS

1. In a medium saucepan, whisk together egg yolks and sugar until well blended. Whisk in milk and cook over medium heat, stirring constantly, until mixture boils. Boil gently for 1 minute, remove from heat and allow to cool slightly. Cover tightly and chill in refrigerator 1 hour.

2. In a medium bowl, beat cream with vanilla until stiff peaks form. Whisk mascarpone into yolk mixture until smooth.

3. In a small bowl, combine coffee and rum. Split ladyfingers in half lengthwise and drizzle with coffee mixture.

4. Arrange half of soaked ladyfingers in bottom of a 7x11 inch dish. Spread half of mascarpone mixture over ladyfingers, then half of whipped cream over that. Repeat layers and sprinkle with cocoa. Cover and refrigerate 4 to 6 hours, until set.

BLUEBERRY PIE
Servings: 8 | Prep: 15m | Cooks: 50m | Total: 1h5m

NUTRITION FACTS

Calories: 366 | Carbohydrates: 52.6g | Fat: 16.6g | Protein: 3.3g | Cholesterol: 4mg

INGREDIENTS

- 3/4 cup white sugar
- 4 cups fresh blueberries
- 3 tablespoons cornstarch
- 1 recipe pastry for a 9 inch double crust pie
- 1/4 teaspoon salt
- 1 tablespoon butter
- 1/2 teaspoon ground cinnamon

DIRECTIONS

1. Preheat oven to 375 degrees F (190 degrees C).
2. Mix sugar, cornstarch, salt, and cinnamon, and sprinkle over blueberries.
3. Line pie dish with one pie crust. Pour berry mixture into the crust, and dot with butter. Cut remaining pastry into 1/2 - 3/4 inch wide strips, and make lattice top. Crimp and flute edges.
4. Bake pie on lower shelf of oven for about 50 minutes, or until crust is golden brown.

DELICIOUS RASPBERRY OATMEAL COOKIE BARS
Servings: 9 | Prep: 15m | Cooks: 40m | Total: 55m

NUTRITION FACTS

Calories: 292 | Carbohydrates: 47g | Fat: 11g | Protein: 2.7g | Cholesterol: 27mg

INGREDIENTS

- 1/2 cup packed light brown sugar
- 1 cup rolled oats
- 1 cup all-purpose flour
- 1/2 cup butter, softened
- 1/4 teaspoon baking soda
- 3/4 cup seedless raspberry jam
- 1/8 teaspoon salt

DIRECTIONS

1. Preheat oven to 350 degrees F (175 degrees C). Grease one 8 inch square pan, and line with greased foil.
2. Combine brown sugar, flour, baking soda, salt, and rolled oats. Rub in the butter using your hands or a pastry blender to form a crumbly mixture. Press 2 cups of the mixture into the bottom of the prepared pan. Spread the jam to within 1/4 inch of the edge. Sprinkle the remaining crumb mixture over the top, and lightly press it into the jam.
3. Bake for 35 to 40 minutes in preheated oven, or until lightly browned. Allow to cool before cutting into bars.

BLONDE BROWNIES

Servings: 6 | Prep: 30m | Cooks: 20m | Total: 50m

NUTRITION FACTS

Calories: 477 | Carbohydrates: 65.4g | Fat: 23.2g | Protein: 5.6g | Cholesterol: 58mg

INGREDIENTS

- 1 cup sifted all-purpose flour
- 1/3 cup butter, melted
- 1/2 teaspoon baking powder
- 1 cup packed brown sugar
- 1/8 teaspoon baking soda
- 1 egg, beaten
- 1/2 teaspoon salt
- 1 tablespoon vanilla extract
- 1/2 cup chopped walnuts
- 2/3 cup semisweet chocolate chips

DIRECTIONS

1. Preheat oven to 350 degrees F (180 degrees C). Grease a 9x9-inch baking pan.
2. Measure 1 cup sifted flour. Add baking powder, baking soda, and salt. Sift again. Add 1/2 cup chopped nuts. Mix well and set aside.
3. Stir the brown sugar into the melted butter and mix well. Cool slightly.
4. Mix the beaten egg and vanilla into the brown sugar mixture. Add flour mixture, a little at a time, mixing just until combined.
5. Spread the batter into the prepared pan. Sprinkle 1/2 to 1 cup chocolate chips on top. Bake in the preheated oven until a toothpick inserted in the center comes out clean, about 20 to 25 minutes.

QUICK AND EASY BROWNIES

Servings: 20 | Prep: 15m | Cooks: 20m | Total: 35m

NUTRITION FACTS

Calories: 229 | Carbohydrates: 28.8g | Fat: 12.2g | Protein: 3.1g | Cholesterol: 62mg

INGREDIENTS

- 1 cup butter, melted
- 1 1/2 cups all-purpose flour
- 2 cups white sugar
- 1/2 teaspoon baking powder
- 1/2 cup cocoa powder
- 1/2 teaspoon salt
- 1 teaspoon vanilla extract
- 1/2 cup walnut halves
- 4 eggs

DIRECTIONS

1. Preheat the oven to 350 degrees F (175 degrees C). Grease a 9x13-inch pan.
2. Combine the melted butter, sugar, cocoa powder, vanilla, eggs, flour, baking powder, and salt. Spread the batter into the prepared pan. Decorate with walnut halves, if desired.
3. Bake in preheated oven for 20 to 30 minutes or until a toothpick inserted in the center comes out with crumbs, not wet. Cool on wire rack.

TIRAMISU LAYER CAKE

Servings: 12 | Prep: 5m | Cooks: 20m | Total: 2h | Additional: 1h35m

Calories: 465 | Carbohydrates: 46.3g | Fat: 28.9g | Protein: 4.4g | Cholesterol: 78mg

INGREDIENTS

- 1 (18.25 ounce) package moist white cake mix
- 2 tablespoons coffee flavored liqueur
- 1 teaspoon instant coffee powder
- 2 cups heavy cream
- 1/4 cup coffee
- 1/4 cup confectioners' sugar
- 1 tablespoon coffee flavored liqueur
- 2 tablespoons coffee flavored liqueur
- 1 (8 ounce) container mascarpone cheese
- 2 tablespoons unsweetened cocoa powder
- 1/2 cup confectioners' sugar
- 1 (1 ounce) square semisweet chocolate

DIRECTIONS

1. Preheat oven to 350 degrees F (175 degrees C). Grease and flour 3 (9 inch) pans.
2. Prepare the cake mix according to package directions. Divide two thirds of batter between 2 pans. Stir instant coffee into remaining batter; pour into remaining pan.
3. Bake in the preheated oven for 20 to 25 minutes, or until a toothpick inserted into the center of the cake comes out clean. Let cool in pan for 10 minutes, then turn out onto a wire rack and cool completely. In a measuring cup, combine brewed coffee and 1 tablespoon coffee liqueur; set aside.
4. To make the filling: In a small bowl, using an electric mixer set on low speed, combine mascarpone, 1/2 cup confectioners' sugar and 2 tablespoons coffee liqueur; beat just until smooth. Cover with plastic wrap and refrigerate.
5. To make the frosting: In a medium bowl, using an electric mixer set on medium-high speed, beat the cream, 1/4 cup confectioners' sugar and 2 tablespoons coffee liqueur until stiff. Fold 1/2 cup of cream mixture into filling mixture.
6. To assemble the cake: Place one plain cake layer on a serving plate. Using a thin skewer, poke holes in cake, about 1 inch apart. Pour one third of reserved coffee mixture over cake, then spread with half of the filling mixture. Top with coffee-flavored cake layer; poke holes in cake. Pour another third of the coffee mixture over the second layer and spread with the remaining filling. Top with remaining cake layer; poke holes in cake. Pour remaining coffee mixture on top. Spread sides and top of cake with frosting. Place cocoa in a sieve and lightly dust top of cake. Garnish with chocolate curls. Refrigerate at least 30 minutes before serving.
7. To make the chocolate curls, use a vegetable peeler and run it down the edge of the chocolate bar.

OLD FASHIONED COCONUT CREAM PIE

Servings: 8 | Prep: 20m | Cooks: 30m | Total: 4h50m | Additional: 4h

NUTRITION FACTS

Calories: 423 | Carbohydrates: 46.1g | Fat: 23.5g | Protein: 6.8g | Cholesterol: 80mg

INGREDIENTS

- 1 cup sweetened flaked coconut
- 1/4 teaspoon salt
- 3 cups half-and-half
- 1 teaspoon vanilla extract
- 2 eggs, beaten
- 1 (9 inch) pie shell, baked
- 3/4 cup white sugar
- 1 cup frozen whipped topping, thawed
- 1/2 cup all-purpose flour

DIRECTIONS

1. Preheat oven to 350 degrees F (175 degrees C).
2. Spread the coconut on a baking sheet and bake it, stirring occasionally, until golden brown, about 5 minutes.
3. In a medium saucepan, combine the half-and-half, eggs, sugar, flour and salt and mix well. Bring to a boil over low heat, stirring constantly. Cook, stirring constantly, for 2 minutes more. Remove the pan from the heat, and stir in 3/4 cup of the toasted coconut and the vanilla extract. Reserve the remaining coconut to top the pie.
4. Pour the filling into the pie shell and chill until firm, about 4 hours.
5. Top with whipped topping and with the reserved coconut.

CHEWY COCONUT COOKIES

Servings: 36 | Prep: 30m | Cooks: 10m | Total: 50m | Additional: 10m

NUTRITION FACTS

Calories: 75 | Carbohydrates: 10.5g | Fat: 3.5g | Protein: 0.7g | Cholesterol: 12mg

INGREDIENTS

- 1 1/4 cups all-purpose flour
- 1/2 cup white sugar
- 1/2 teaspoon baking soda

- 1 egg
- 1/4 teaspoon salt
- 1/2 teaspoon vanilla extract
- 1/2 cup butter
- 1 1/3 cups flaked coconut
- 1/2 cup packed brown sugar

DIRECTIONS

1. Preheat oven to 350 degrees F (175 degrees C.) Combine the flour, baking soda, and salt; set aside.
2. In a medium bowl, cream the butter, brown sugar, and white sugar until smooth. Beat in the egg and vanilla until light and fluffy. Gradually blend in the flour mixture, then mix in the coconut. Drop dough by teaspoonfuls onto an ungreased cookie sheet. Cookies should be about 3 inches apart.
3. Bake for 8 to 10 minutes in the preheated oven, or until lightly toasted. Cool on wire racks.

GOLDEN RUM CAKE

Servings: 12 | Prep: 30m | Cooks: 1h | Total: 1h30m

NUTRITION FACTS

Calories: 562 | Carbohydrates: 59.2g | Fat: 29.9g | Protein: 5.6g | Cholesterol: 83mg

INGREDIENTS

- 1 cup chopped walnuts
- 1/2 cup dark rum
- 1 (18.25 ounce) package yellow cake mix
- 1/2 cup butter
- 1 (3.4 ounce) package instant vanilla pudding mix
- 1/4 cup water
- 4 eggs
- 1 cup white sugar
- 1/2 cup water
- 1/2 cup dark rum
- 1/2 cup vegetable oil

DIRECTIONS

1. Preheat oven to 325 degrees F (165 degrees C). Grease and flour a 10 inch Bundt pan. Sprinkle chopped nuts evenly over the bottom of the pan.
2. In a large bowl, combine cake mix and pudding mix. Mix in the eggs, 1/2 cup water, oil and 1/2 cup rum. Blend well. Pour batter over chopped nuts in the pan.

3. Bake in the preheated oven for 60 minutes, or until a toothpick inserted into the cake comes out clean. Let sit for 10 minutes in the pan, then turn out onto serving plate. Brush glaze over top and sides. Allow cake to absorb glaze and repeat until all glaze is used.

4. To make the glaze: in a saucepan, combine butter, 1/4 cup water and 1 cup sugar. Bring to a boil over medium heat and continue to boil for 5 minutes, stirring constantly. Remove from heat and stir in 1/2 cup rum.

BETTER BROWNIES

Servings: 16 | Prep: 15m | Cooks: 25m | Total: 40m

NUTRITION FACTS

Calories: 161 | Carbohydrates: 17.1g | Fat: 10.2g | Protein: 2.1g | Cholesterol: 23mg

INGREDIENTS

- 1/2 cup vegetable oil
- 1/3 cup unsweetened cocoa powder
- 1 cup white sugar
- 1/4 teaspoon baking powder
- 1 teaspoon vanilla extract
- 1/4 teaspoon salt
- 2 eggs
- 1/2 cup chopped walnuts (optional)
- 1/2 cup all-purpose flour

DIRECTIONS

1. Preheat oven to 350 degrees F (175 degrees C). Grease a 9x9 inch baking pan.

2. In a medium bowl, mix together the oil, sugar, and vanilla. Beat in eggs. Combine flour, cocoa, baking powder, and salt; gradually stir into the egg mixture until well blended. Stir in walnuts, if desired. Spread the batter evenly into the prepared pan.

3. Bake for 20 to 25 minutes, or until the brownie begins to pull away from edges of pan. Let cool on a wire rack before cutting into squares.

BEST CARROT CAKE EVER

Servings: 16 | Prep: 1h30m | Cooks: 1h | Total: 2h30m

NUTRITION FACTS

Calories: 457 | Carbohydrates: 66.3g | Fat: 20.2g | Protein: 5.9g | Cholesterol: 47mg

INGREDIENTS

* 6 cups grated carrots
* 1 cup crushed pineapple, drained
* 1 cup brown sugar
* 3 cups all-purpose flour
* 1 cup raisins
* 1 1/2 teaspoons baking soda
* 4 eggs
* 1 teaspoon salt
* 1 1/2 cups white sugar
* 4 teaspoons ground cinnamon
* 1 cup vegetable oil
* 1 cup chopped walnuts
* 2 teaspoons vanilla extract

DIRECTIONS

1. In a medium bowl, combine grated carrots and brown sugar. Set aside for 60 minutes, then stir in raisins.
2. Preheat oven to 350 degrees F (175 degrees C). Grease and flour two 10 inch cake pans.
3. In a large bowl, beat eggs until light. Gradually beat in the white sugar, oil and vanilla. Stir in the pineapple. Combine the flour, baking soda, salt and cinnamon, stir into the wet mixture until absorbed. Finally stir in the carrot mixture and the walnuts. Pour evenly into the prepared pans.
4. Bake for 45 to 50 minutes in the preheated oven, until cake tests done with a toothpick. Cool for 10 minutes before removing from pan. When completely cooled, frost with cream cheese frosting.

DAVID'S YELLOW CAKE

Servings: 12 | Prep: 20m | Cooks: 30m | Total: 50m

NUTRITION FACTS

Calories: 360 | Carbohydrates: 44.2g | Fat: 18.8g | Protein: 4.3g | Cholesterol: 178mg

INGREDIENTS

* 1 cup butter
* 1 1/2 teaspoons vanilla extract
* 1 1/2 cups white sugar
* 2 cups cake flour
* 8 egg yolks
* 2 teaspoons baking powder

- 3/4 cup milk
- 1/2 teaspoon salt

DIRECTIONS

1. Preheat oven to 350 degrees F (175 degrees C). Grease and flour 2 - 8 inch round pans. Sift together the flour, baking powder and salt. Set aside.
2. In a large bowl, cream together the butter and sugar until light and fluffy. Beat in the egg yolks one at a time, then stir in the vanilla. Beat in the flour mixture alternately with the milk, mixing just until incorporated. Pour batter into prepared pans.
3. Bake in the preheated oven for 25 to 30 minutes, or until tops spring back when lightly tapped. Cool 15 minutes before turning out onto cooling racks.

CHOCOLATE ECLAIR DESSERT
Servings: 12 | Prep: 15m | Cooks: 2h | Total: 2h15m

NUTRITION FACTS

Calories: 401 | Carbohydrates: 65.6g | Fat: 13.7g | Protein: 4.2g | Cholesterol: 5mg

INGREDIENTS

- 2 individual packages graham crackers
- 1 (8 ounce) container frozen whipped topping, thawed
- 2 (3 ounce) packages instant vanilla pudding mix
- 1 (16 ounce) package prepared chocolate frosting
- 3 cups milk

DIRECTIONS

1. Line the bottom of a 9x13-inch pan with graham crackers.
2. In a large bowl, combine pudding mix and milk; stir well. Mix whipped topping into pudding mixture. Spread half of mixture over graham cracker layer. Top with another layer of graham crackers and the remaining pudding.
3. Top all with a final layer of graham crackers and frost with chocolate frosting. Refrigerate at least two hours before serving to allow the graham crackers to soften.

CREAM CHEESE POUND CAKE
Servings: 4 | Prep: 30m | Cooks: 1h | Total: 1h30m

NUTRITION FACTS

Calories: 525 | Carbohydrates: 63.9g | Fat: 27.7g | Protein: 6.9g | Cholesterol: 150mg

INGREDIENTS

- 1 (8 ounce) package cream cheese
- 6 eggs
- 1 1/2 cups butter
- 3 cups all-purpose flour
- 3 cups white sugar
- 1 teaspoon vanilla extract

DIRECTIONS

1. Preheat oven to 325 degrees F (160 degrees C) grease and flour a 10 inch tube pan.
2. In a large bowl, cream butter and cream cheese until smooth. Add sugar gradually and beat until fluffy.
3. Add eggs two at a time, beating well with each addition. Add the flour all at once and mix in. Add vanilla.
4. Pour into a 10 inch tube pan. Bake at 325 degrees F (160 degrees C) for 1 hour and 20 minutes. Check for doneness at 1 hour. A toothpick inserted into center of cake will come out clean.

CHOCOLATE CORNSTARCH PUDDING

Servings: 4 | Prep: 10m | Cooks: 20m | Total: 40m

NUTRITION FACTS

Calories: 274 | Carbohydrates: 42.5g | Fat: 9.6g | Protein: 6.4g | Cholesterol: 29mg

INGREDIENTS

- 1/2 cup white sugar
- 2 3/4 cups milk
- 3 tablespoons unsweetened cocoa powder
- 2 tablespoons butter, room temperature
- 1/4 cup cornstarch
- 1 teaspoon vanilla extract
- 1/8 teaspoon salt

DIRECTIONS

1. In a saucepan, stir together sugar, cocoa, cornstarch and salt. Place over medium heat, and stir in milk. Bring to a boil, and cook, stirring constantly, until mixture thickens enough to coat the back of a metal spoon. Remove from heat, and stir in butter and vanilla. Let cool briefly, and serve warm, or chill in refrigerator until serving.

MY AMISH FRIEND'S CARAMEL CORN

Servings: 28 | Prep: 15m | Cooks: 1h | Total: 1h15m

NUTRITION FACTS

Calories: 238 | Carbohydrates: 21.9g | Fat: 16.3g | Protein: 3.4g | Cholesterol: 0mg

INGREDIENTS

- 7 quarts plain popped popcorn
- 1 teaspoon salt
- 2 cups dry roasted peanuts (optional)
- 1 cup margarine
- 2 cups brown sugar
- 1/2 teaspoon baking soda
- 1/2 cup light corn syrup
- 1 teaspoon vanilla extract

DIRECTIONS

1. Place the popped popcorn into two shallow greased baking pans. You may use roasting pans, jelly roll pans, or disposable roasting pans. Add the peanuts to the popped corn if using. Set aside.
2. Preheat the oven to 250 degrees F (120 degrees C). Combine the brown sugar, corn syrup, margarine and salt in a saucepan. Bring to a boil over medium heat, stirring enough to blend. Once the mixture begins to boil, boil for 5 minutes while stirring constantly.
3. Remove from the heat, and stir in the baking soda and vanilla. The mixture will be light and foamy. Immediately pour over the popcorn in the pans, and stir to coat. Don't worry too much at this point about getting all of the corn coated.
4. Bake for 1 hour, removing the pans, and giving them each a good stir every 15 minutes. Line the counter top with waxed paper. Dump the corn out onto the waxed paper and separate the pieces. Allow to cool completely, then store in airtight containers or resealable bags.

COCONUT MACAROONS

Servings: 12 | Prep: 10m | Cooks: 35m | Total: 25m | Additional: 15m

NUTRITION FACTS

Calories: 287 | Carbohydrates: 40.7g | Fat: 12.4g | Protein: 4.4g | Cholesterol: 11mg

INGREDIENTS

- 2/3 cup all-purpose flour
- 1 (14 ounce) can sweetened condensed milk
- 5 1/2 cups flaked coconut
- 2 teaspoons vanilla extract

- 1/4 teaspoon salt

DIRECTIONS

1. Preheat oven to 350 degrees F (175 degrees C). Line cookie sheets with parchment paper or aluminum foil.
2. In a large bowl, stir together the flour, coconut and salt. Stir in the sweetened condensed milk and vanilla using your hands until well blended. Use an ice cream scoop to drop dough onto the prepared cookie sheets. Cookies should be about golf ball size.
3. Bake for 12 to 15 minutes in the preheated oven, until coconut is toasted.

APPLE SQUARES

Servings: 16 | Prep: 25m | Cooks: 30m | Total: 55m

NUTRITION FACTS

Calories: 143 | Carbohydrates: 22.1g | Fat: 5.7g | Protein: 1.8g | Cholesterol: 19mg

INGREDIENTS

- 1 cup sifted all-purpose flour
- 1 egg
- 1 teaspoon baking powder
- 1 teaspoon vanilla extract
- 1/4 teaspoon salt
- 1/2 cup chopped apple
- 1/4 teaspoon ground cinnamon
- 1/2 cup finely chopped walnuts
- 1/4 cup butter or margarine, melted
- 2 tablespoons white sugar
- 1/2 cup packed brown sugar
- 2 teaspoons ground cinnamon
- 1/2 cup white sugar

DIRECTIONS

1. Preheat oven to 350 degrees F (175 degrees C). Grease a 9x9 inch pan. Sift together flour, baking powder, salt, and 1/4 teaspoon of cinnamon; set aside.
2. In a large bowl, mix together melted butter, brown sugar, and 1/2 cup of white sugar with a wooden spoon until smooth. Stir in the egg and vanilla. Blend in the flour mixture until just combined, then stir in the apples and walnuts. Spread the mixture evenly into the prepared pan. In a cup or small bowl, stir together the remaining cinnamon and sugar; sprinkle over the top of the bars.

CREAM PUFFS

Servings: 20 | Prep: 30m | Cooks: 25m | Total: 55m

NUTRITION FACTS

Calories: 190 | Carbohydrates: 15.2g | Fat: 13.3g | Protein: 2.9g | Cholesterol: 77mg

INGREDIENTS

- 2 (3.5 ounce) packages instant vanilla pudding mix
- 1 cup water
- 2 cups heavy cream
- 1/4 teaspoon salt
- 1 cup milk
- 1 cup all-purpose flour
- 1/2 cup butter
- 4 eggs

DIRECTIONS

1. Mix together vanilla instant pudding mix, cream and milk. Cover and refrigerate to set.
2. Preheat oven to 425 degrees F (220 degrees C).
3. In a large pot, bring water and butter to a rolling boil. Stir in flour and salt until the mixture forms a ball. Transfer the dough to a large mixing bowl. Using a wooden spoon or stand mixer, beat in the eggs one at a time, mixing well after each. Drop by tablespoonfuls onto an ungreased baking sheet.
4. Bake for 20 to 25 minutes in the preheated oven, until golden brown. Centers should be dry.
5. When the shells are cool, either split and fill them with the pudding mixture, or use a pastry bag to pipe the pudding into the shells.

MELT - IN - YOUR - MOUTH SHORTBREAD

Servings: 24 | Prep: 10m | Cooks: 15m | Total: 25m

NUTRITION FACTS

Calories: 111 | Carbohydrates: 9.7g | Fat: 7.8g | Protein: 0.9g | Cholesterol: 20mg

INGREDIENTS

- 1 cup butter, softened
- 1/4 cup cornstarch
- 1/2 cup confectioners' sugar
- 1 1/2 cups all-purpose flour

DIRECTIONS

1. Preheat the oven to 375 degrees F (190 degrees C).

2. Whip butter with an electric mixer until fluffy. Stir in the confectioners' sugar, cornstarch, and flour. Beat on low for one minute, then on high for 3 to 4 minutes. Drop cookies by spoonfuls 2 inches apart on an ungreased cookie sheet.

3. Bake for 12 to 15 minutes in the preheated oven. Watch that the edges don't brown too much. Cool on wire racks.

RED VELVET CUPCAKES

Servings: 30 | Prep: 20m | Cooks: 20m | Total: 40m

NUTRITION FACTS

Calories: 276 | Carbohydrates: 37.8g | Fat: 13.1g | Protein: 3.2g | Cholesterol: 57mg

INGREDIENTS

- 2 1/2 cups flour
- 1/2 cup milk
- 1/2 cup unsweetened cocoa powder
- 1 (1 ounce) bottle McCormick Red Food Color
- 1 teaspoon baking soda
- 2 teaspoons McCormick Pure Vanilla Extract
- 1/2 teaspoon salt
- 1 (8 ounce) package cream cheese, softened
- 1 cup butter, softened
- 1/4 cup butter, softened
- 2 cups sugar
- 2 tablespoons sour cream
- 4 eggs
- 2 teaspoons McCormick Pure Vanilla Extract
- 1 cup sour cream
- 1 (16 ounce) box confectioners' sugar

DIRECTIONS

1. Preheat oven to 350 degrees F. Mix flour, cocoa powder, baking soda and salt in medium bowl. Set aside.
2. Beat butter and sugar in large bowl with electric mixer on medium speed 5 minutes or until light and fluffy. Beat in eggs, one at a time. Mix in sour cream, milk, food color and vanilla. Gradually beat in flour mixture on low speed until just blended. Do not overbeat. Spoon batter into 30 paper-lined muffin cups, filling each cup 2/3 full.
3. Bake 20 minutes or until toothpick inserted into cupcake comes out clean. Cool in pans on wire rack 5 minutes. Remove from pans; cool completely. Frost with Vanilla Cream Cheese Frosting.

4. Vanilla Cream Cheese Frosting: Beat cream cheese, softened, butter, sour cream and McCormick(R) Pure Vanilla Extract in large bowl until light and fluffy. Gradually beat in confectioners' sugar until smooth.

EASY KEY LIME PIE

Servings: 8 | Prep: 20m | Cooks: 15m | Total: 35m

NUTRITION FACTS

Calories: 324 | Carbohydrates: 45.5g | Fat: 13.6g | Protein: 6.7g | Cholesterol: 145mg

INGREDIENTS

- 5 egg yolks, beaten
- 1/2 cup key lime juice
- 1 (14 ounce) can sweetened condensed milk
- 1 (9 inch) prepared graham cracker crust

DIRECTIONS

1. Preheat oven to 375 degrees F (190 degrees C).
2. Combine the egg yolks, sweetened condensed milk and lime juice. Mix well. Pour into unbaked graham cracker shell.
3. Bake in preheated oven for 15 minutes. Allow to cool. Top with whipped topping and garnish with lime slices if desired.

PAUL'S PUMPKIN BARS

Servings: 24 | Prep: 15m | Cooks: 30m | Total: 45m

NUTRITION FACTS

Calories: 279 | Carbohydrates: 34.1g | Fat: 15.2g | Protein: 2.6g | Cholesterol: 45mg

INGREDIENTS

- 4 eggs
- 1 teaspoon baking soda
- 1 2/3 cups white sugar
- 2 teaspoons ground cinnamon
- 1 cup vegetable oil
- 1 teaspoon salt
- 1 (15 ounce) can pumpkin puree

- 1 (3 ounce) package cream cheese, softened
- 2 cups all-purpose flour
- 1/2 cup butter, softened
- 2 teaspoons baking powder
- 1 teaspoon vanilla extra
- 2 cups sifted confectioners' sugar

DIRECTIONS

1. Preheat oven to 350 degrees F (175 degrees C).
2. In a medium bowl, mix the eggs, sugar, oil, and pumpkin with an electric mixer until light and fluffy. Sift together the flour, baking powder, baking soda, cinnamon and salt. Stir into the pumpkin mixture until thoroughly combined.
3. Spread the batter evenly into an ungreased 10x15 inch jellyroll pan. Bake for 25 to 30 minutes in preheated oven. Cool before frosting.
4. To make the frosting, cream together the cream cheese and butter. Stir in vanilla. Add confectioners' sugar a little at a time, beating until mixture is smooth. Spread evenly on top of the cooled bars. Cut into squares.

EILEEN'S SPICY GINGERBREAD MENS

Servings: 30 | Prep: 20m | Cooks: 10m | Total: 30m

NUTRITION FACTS

Calories: 88 | Carbohydrates: 14g | Fat: 3.3g | Protein: 1g | Cholesterol: 7mg

INGREDIENTS

- 1/2 cup margarine
- 1/2 teaspoon baking powder
- 1/2 cup sugar
- 1/2 teaspoon baking soda
- 1/2 cup molasses
- 1/2 teaspoon ground cinnamon
- 1 egg yolk
- 1 teaspoon ground cloves
- 2 cups sifted all-purpose flour
- 1 teaspoon ginger
- 1/2 teaspoon salt
- 1/2 teaspoon ground nutmeg

DIRECTIONS

1. In a large bowl, cream together the margarine and sugar until smooth. Stir in molasses and egg yolk. Combine the flour, salt, baking powder, baking soda, cinnamon, cloves, ginger, and nutmeg; blend into the molasses mixture until smooth. Cover, and chill for at least one hour.
2. Preheat the oven to 350 degrees F (175 degrees C). On a lightly floured surface, roll the dough out to 1/4 inch thickness. Cut into desired shapes with cookie cutters. Place cookies 2 inches apart on ungreased cookie sheets.
3. Bake for 8 to 10 minutes in the preheated oven, until firm. Remove from cookie sheets to cool on wire racks. Frost or decorate when cool.

ABSOLUTELY THE BEST CHOCOLATE CHIP COOKIES
Servings: 24 | Prep: 10m | Cooks: 10m | Total: 20m

NUTRITION FACTS

Calories: 241 | Carbohydrates: 28.1g | Fat: 13.7g | Protein: 2.7g | Cholesterol: 20mg

INGREDIENTS

- 1 cup butter flavored shortening
- 21/4 cups all-purpose flour
- 3/4 cup white sugar
- 1 teaspoon baking soda
- 3/4 cup brown sugar
- 1 teaspoon salt
- 2 eggs
- 2 cups milk chocolate chips
- 2 teaspoons Mexican vanilla extract

DIRECTIONS

1. Preheat oven to 350 degrees F (175 degrees C). Grease cookie sheets.
2. In a large bowl, cream together the butter flavored shortening, brown sugar and white sugar until light and fluffy. Add the eggs one at a time, beating well with each addition, then stir in the vanilla .Combine the flour, baking soda and salt; gradually stir into the creamed mixture. Finally, fold in the chocolate chips. Drop by rounded spoonfuls onto the prepared cookie sheets.
3. Bake for 8 to 10 minutes in the preheated oven, until light brown. Allow cookies to cool on baking sheet for 5 minutes before removing to a wire rack to cool completely.

CHOCOLATE CUPCAKES
Servings: 16 | Prep: 15m | Cooks: 15m | Total: 30m

NUTRITION FACTS

Calories: 158 | Carbohydrates: 29.8g | Fat: 3.9g | Protein: 3.2g | Cholesterol: 30mg

INGREDIENTS

- 1 1/3 cups all-purpose flour
- 3 tablespoons butter, softened
- 1/4 teaspoon baking soda
- 1 1/2 cups white sugar
- 2 teaspoons baking powder
- 2 eggs
- 3/4 cup unsweetened cocoa powder
- 3/4 teaspoon vanilla extract
- 1/8 teaspoon salt
- 1 cup milk

DIRECTIONS

1. Preheat oven to 350 degrees F (175 degrees C). Line a muffin pan with paper or foil liners. Sift together the flour, baking powder, baking soda, cocoa and salt. Set aside.
2. In a large bowl, cream together the butter and sugar until light and fluffy. Add the eggs one at a time, beating well with each addition, then stir in the vanilla. Add the flour mixture alternately with the milk; beat well. Fill the muffin cups 3/4 full.
3. Bake for 15 to 17 minutes in the preheated oven, or until a toothpick inserted into the cake comes out clean. Frost with your favorite frosting when cool.

ANNA'S CHOCOLATE CHIP COOKIES
Servings: 48 | Prep: 15m | Cooks: 10m | Total: 25m

NUTRITION FACTS

Calories: 120 | Carbohydrates: 16g | Fat: 6.2g | Protein: 1.3g | Cholesterol: 18mg

INGREDIENTS

- 1 cup butter
- 2 1/2 cups all-purpose flour
- 1/2 cup white sugar
- 1 teaspoon baking soda
- 1 cup packed brown sugar
- 1 teaspoon salt
- 1 teaspoon vanilla extract

- 2 cups semisweet chocolate chips
- 2 eggs

DIRECTIONS

1. Preheat the oven to 375 degrees F (190 degrees C)
2. In a large bowl, cream together the butter and sugar until smooth. Beat in the vanilla and eggs one at a time. Combine the flour, baking soda and salt; stir into the sugar mixture. Finally, mix in the chocolate chips. Drop by tablespoonfuls onto ungreased cookie sheets.
3. Bake for 8 to 10 minutes in the preheated oven, or until edges are golden. Remove from baking sheet to cool on wire racks.

CRUSTLESS CRANBERRY PIE
Servings: 8 | Prep: 15m | Cooks: 40m | Total: 55m

NUTRITION FACTS

Calories: 335 | Carbohydrates: 41.4g | Fat: 17.7g | Protein: 4.5g | Cholesterol: 77mg

INGREDIENTS

- 1 cup all-purpose flour
- 1/2 cup chopped walnuts
- 1 cup white sugar
- 1/2 cup butter, melted
- 1/4 teaspoon salt
- 2 eggs
- 2 cups cranberries
- 1 teaspoon almond extract

DIRECTIONS

1. Preheat oven to 350 degrees F (175 degrees C). Grease one 9 inch pie pan.
2. Combine the flour, sugar, and salt. Stir in the cranberries and the walnuts, and toss to coat. Stir in the butter, beaten eggs, and almond extract. If you are using frozen cranberries, the mixture will be very thick. Spread the batter into the prepared pan.
3. Bake at 350 degrees F (175 degrees C) for 40 minutes, or until a wooden pick inserted near the center comes out clean. Serve warm with whipped cream or ice cream.

OATMEAL PEANUT BUTTER COOKIES
Servings: 12 | Prep: 30m | Cooks: 10m | Total: 40m

Calories: 397 | Carbohydrates: 42.2g | Fat: 23.5g | Protein: 7.8g | Cholesterol: 48mg

INGREDIENTS

- 3/4 cup all-purpose flour
- 1 egg
- 1/2 teaspoon baking soda
- 1 teaspoon vanilla extract
- 1/4 teaspoon baking powder
- 1 cup quick cooking oats
- 1/2 teaspoon salt
- 3 tablespoons butter, softened
- 1/2 cup butter, softened
- 1 cup confectioners' sugar
- 1/2 cup peanut butter
- 1/2 cup smooth peanut butter
- 1/2 cup white sugar
- 2 1/2 tablespoons heavy whipping cream
- 1/2 cup packed light brown sugar

DIRECTIONS

1. In a large bowl, cream together 1/2 cup butter or margarine, 1/2 cup peanut butter, white sugar, brown sugar, and vanilla. Add egg and beat well.
2. In another bowl, combine the flour, baking soda, baking powder, and salt. Add these dry ingredients to the creamed mixture. Stir. Add oatmeal and stir.
3. Drop by teaspoons onto greased baking sheet, and press each mound down with a fork to form 1/4 inch thick cookies. Bake at 350 degrees F (175 degrees C) for 10 minutes, or until cookies are a light brown.
4. To Make Filling: Cream 3 tablespoons butter or margarine with the confectioners' sugar, 1/2 cup smooth peanut butter, and the cream. Spread filling onto half of the cooled cookies, then top with the other half to form sandwiches.

TRIPLE BERRY CRISP

Servings: 18 | Prep: 20m | Cooks: 40m | Total: 1h

NUTRITION FACTS

Calories: 295 | Carbohydrates: 35.6g | Fat: 16.3g | Protein: 3.2g | Cholesterol: 41mg

INGREDIENTS

- 1 1/2 cups fresh blackberries
- 2 cups rolled oats
- 1 1/2 cups fresh raspberries
- 1 1/2 cups packed brown sugar
- 1 1/2 cups fresh blueberries
- 1 teaspoon ground cinnamon
- 4 tablespoons white sugar
- 1/2 teaspoon ground nutmeg
- 2 cups all-purpose flour
- 1 1/2 cups butter

DIRECTIONS

1. Preheat oven to 350 degrees F (175 degrees C).
2. In a large bowl, gently toss together blackberries, raspberries, blueberries, and white sugar; set aside.
3. In a separate large bowl, combine flour, oats, brown sugar, cinnamon, and nutmeg. Cut in butter until crumbly. Press half of mixture in the bottom of a 9x13 inch pan. Cover with berries. Sprinkle remaining crumble mixture over the berries.
4. Bake in the preheated oven for 30 to 40 minutes, or until fruit is bubbly and topping is golden brown.

BLUEBERRY SOUR CREAM COFFEE CAKE

Servings: 12 | Prep: 20m | Cooks: 1h | Total: 1h

NUTRITION FACTS

Calories: 459 | Carbohydrates: 59.5g | Fat: 24g | Protein: 4.1g | Cholesterol: 80mg

INGREDIENTS

- 1 cup butter, softened
- 1/4 teaspoon salt
- 2 cups white sugar
- 1 cup fresh or frozen blueberries
- 2 eggs
- 1/2 cup brown sugar
- 1 cup sour cream
- 1 teaspoon ground cinnamon
- 1 teaspoon vanilla extract
- 1/2 cup chopped pecans
- 1 5/8 cups all-purpose flour
- 1 tablespoon confectioners' sugar for dusting

- 1 teaspoon baking powder

DIRECTIONS

1. Preheat the oven to 350 degrees F (175 degrees C). Grease and flour a 9 inch Bundt pan.
2. In a large bowl, cream together the butter and sugar until light and fluffy. Beat in the eggs one at a time, then stir in the sour cream and vanilla. Combine the flour, baking powder, and salt; stir into the batter just until blended. Fold in blueberries.
3. Spoon half of the batter into the prepared pan. In a small bowl, stir together the brown sugar, cinnamon and pecans. Sprinkle half of this mixture over the batter in the pan. Spoon remaining batter over the top, and then sprinkle the remaining pecan mixture over. Use a knife or thin spatula to swirl the sugar layer into the cake.
4. Bake for 55 to 60 minutes in the preheated oven, or until a knife inserted into the crown of the cake comes out clean. Cool in the pan over a wire rack. Invert onto a serving plate, and tap firmly to remove from the pan. Dust with confectioners' sugar just before serving.

BEST TOFFEE EVER - SUPER EASY
Servings: 32 | Prep: 5m | Cooks: 15m | Total: 1h20m

NUTRITION FACTS

Calories: 226 | Carbohydrates: 20g | Fat: 16.9g | Protein: 1.5g | Cholesterol: 31mg

INGREDIENTS

- 2 cups butter
- 2 cups semisweet chocolate chips
- 2 cups white sugar
- 1 cup finely chopped almonds
- 1/4 teaspoon salt

DIRECTIONS

1. In a large heavy bottomed saucepan, combine the butter, sugar and salt. Cook over medium heat, stirring until the butter is melted. Allow to come to a boil, and cook until the mixture becomes a dark amber color, and the temperature has reached 285 degrees F (137 degrees C). Stir occasionally.
2. While the toffee is cooking, cover a large baking sheet with aluminum foil or parchment paper.
3. As soon as the toffee reaches the proper temperature, pour it out onto the prepared baking sheet. Sprinkle the chocolate over the top, and let it set for a minute or two to soften. Spread the chocolate into a thin even layer once it is melted. Sprinkle the nuts over the chocolate, and press in slightly. Putting a plastic bag over your hand will minimize the mess.
4. Place the toffee in the refrigerator to chill until set. Break into pieces, and store in an airtight container.

BETTER THAN SEX CAKE

Servings: 24 | Prep: 30m | Cooks: 1h | Total: 1h30m

NUTRITION FACTS

Calories: 193 | Carbohydrates: 29.3g | Fat: 7.6g | Protein: 2.7g | Cholesterol: 10mg

INGREDIENTS

- 1 (18.25 ounce) package devil's food cake mix
- 3 (1.4 ounce) bars chocolate covered toffee, chopped
- 1/2 (14 ounce) can sweetened condensed milk
- 1 (8 ounce) container frozen whipped topping, thawed
- 6 ounces caramel ice cream topping

DIRECTIONS

1. Bake cake according to package directions for a 9x13 inch pan; cool on wire rack for 5 minutes. Make slits across the top of the cake, making sure not to go through to the bottom.
2. In a saucepan over low heat, combine sweetened condensed milk and caramel topping, stirring until smooth and blended. Slowly pour the warm topping mixture over the top of the warm cake, letting it sink into the slits; then sprinkle the crushed chocolate toffee bars liberally across the entire cake while still warm. (Hint: I crush my candy bars into small chunks as opposed to crumbs - I like to have pieces I can chew on!)
3. Let cake cool completely, then top with whipped topping. Decorate the top of the cake with some more chocolate toffee bar chunks and swirls of caramel topping. Refrigerate and serve right from the pan!

BAKE SALE LEMON BARS

Servings: 36 | Prep: 15m | Cooks: 45m | Total: 1h

NUTRITION FACTS

Calories: 107 | Carbohydrates: 16.3g | Fat: 4.3g | Protein: 1.2g | Cholesterol: 26mg

INGREDIENTS

- 1 1/2 cups all-purpose flour
- 1 1/2 cups white sugar
- 2/3 cup confectioners' sugar
- 3 tablespoons all-purpose flour
- 3/4 cup butter or margarine, softened
- 1/4 cup lemon juice

- 3 eggs
- 1/3 cup confectioners' sugar for decoration

DIRECTIONS

1. Preheat the oven to 375 degrees F (190 degrees C). Grease a 9x13 inch baking pan.
2. Combine the flour, 2/3 cup confectioners' sugar, and butter. Pat dough into prepared pan.
3. Bake for 20 minutes in the preheated oven, until slightly golden. While the crust is baking, whisk together eggs, white sugar, flour, and lemon juice until frothy. Pour this lemon mixture over the hot crust.
4. Return to the preheated oven for an additional 20 to 25 minutes, or until light golden brown. Cool on a wire rack. Dust the top with confectioners' sugar. Cut into squares.

CRANBERRY ORANGE COOKIES

Servings: 48 | Prep: 20m | Cooks: 14m | Total: 34m

NUTRITION FACTS

Calories: 110 | Carbohydrates: 16.2g | Fat: 4.8g | Protein: 1.1g | Cholesterol: 14mg

INGREDIENTS

- 1 cup butter, softened
- 1/2 teaspoon baking soda
- 1 cup white sugar
- 1/2 teaspoon salt
- 1/2 cup packed brown sugar
- 2 cups chopped cranberries
- 1 egg
- 1/2 cup chopped walnuts (optional)
- 1 teaspoon grated orange zest
- 1/2 teaspoon grated orange zest
- 2 tablespoons orange juice
- 3 tablespoons orange juice
- 2 1/2 cups all-purpose flour
- 1 1/2 cups confectioners' sugar

DIRECTIONS

1. Preheat the oven to 375 degrees F (190 degrees C).
2. In a large bowl, cream together the butter, white sugar and brown sugar until smooth. Beat in the egg until well blended. Mix in 1 teaspoon orange zest and 2 tablespoons orange juice. Combine the flour,

baking soda and salt; stir into the orange mixture. Mix in cranberries and if using, walnuts, until evenly distributed. Drop dough by rounded tablespoonfuls onto ungreased cookie sheets. Cookies should be spaced at least 2 inches apart.

3. Bake for 12 to 14 minutes in the preheated oven, until the edges are golden. Remove from cookie sheets to cool on wire racks.

4. In a small bowl, mix together 1/2 teaspoon orange zest, 3 tablespoons orange juice and confectioners' sugar until smooth. Spread over the tops of cooled cookies. Let stand until set.

LIBBY'S FAMOUS PUMPKIN PIE
Servings: 8 | Prep: 10m | Cooks: 1h | Total: 1h10m

NUTRITION FACTS

Calories: 283 | Carbohydrates: 38.7g | Fat: 12.1g | Protein: 6.4g | Cholesterol: 59mg

INGREDIENTS

- 1 (9 inch) unbaked deep dish pie crust
- 1/4 teaspoon ground cloves
- 3/4 cup white sugar
- 2 eggs
- 1 teaspoon ground cinnamon
- 1 (15 ounce) can LIBBY'S 100% Pure Pumpkin
- 1/2 teaspoon salt
- 1 (12 fluid ounce) can NESTLE CARNATION Evaporated Milk
- 1/2 teaspoon ground ginger

DIRECTIONS

5. Preheat oven to 425 degrees F.

1. Combine sugar, salt, cinnamon, ginger and cloves in small bowl. Beat eggs lightly in large bowl. Stir in pumpkin and sugar-spice mixture. Gradually stir in evaporated milk. Pour into pie shell.
2. Bake for 15 minutes. Reduce temperature to 350 degrees F.; bake for 40 to 50 minutes or until knife inserted near center comes out clean. Cool on wire rack for 2 hours. Serve immediately or refrigerate. (Do not freeze as this will cause the crust to separate from the filling.)

MICROWAVE CHOCOLATE MUG CAKE
Servings: 1 | Prep: 5m | Cooks: 2m | Total: 7m

NUTRITION FACTS

Calories: 603 | Carbohydrates: 82g | Fat: 30.4g | Protein: 6.9g | Cholesterol: 4mg

INGREDIENTS

- 1/4 cup all-purpose flour
- 3 tablespoons milk
- 1/4 cup white sugar
- 2 tablespoons canola oil
- 2 tablespoons unsweetened cocoa powder
- 1 tablespoon water
- 1/8 teaspoon baking soda
- 1/4 teaspoon vanilla extract
- 1/8 teaspoon salt

DIRECTIONS

1. Mix flour, sugar, cocoa powder, baking soda, and salt in a large microwave-safe mug; stir in milk, canola oil, water, and vanilla extract.
2. Cook in microwave until cake is done in the middle, about 1 minute 45 seconds.

JAM FILLED BUTTER COOKIES

Servings: 36 | Prep: 30m | Cooks: 10m | Total: 40m

NUTRITION FACTS

Calories: 82 | Carbohydrates: 10.5g | Fat: 4.1g | Protein: 0.8g | Cholesterol: 22mg

INGREDIENTS

- 3/4 cup butter, softened
- 1 3/4 cups all-purpose flour
- 1/2 cup white sugar
- 1/2 cup fruit preserves, any flavor
- 2 egg yolks

DIRECTIONS

1. Preheat the oven to 375 degrees F (190 degrees C).
2. In a medium bowl, cream together the butter, white sugar and egg yolks. Mix in flour a little bit at a time until a soft dough forms. Roll dough into 1 inch balls. If dough is too soft, refrigerate for 15 to 20 minutes. Place balls 2 inches apart onto ungreased cookie sheets. Use your finger or an instrument of similar size to make a well in the center of each cookie. Fill the hole with 1/2 teaspoon of preserves.

3. Bake for 8 to 10 minutes in the preheated oven, until golden brown on the bottom. Remove from cookie sheets to cool on wire racks.

BEST PEANUT BRITTLE

Servings: 16 | Prep: 10m | Cooks: 15m | Total: 55m

NUTRITION FACTS

Calories: 143 | Carbohydrates: 22.3g | Fat: 6g | Protein: 2.2g | Cholesterol: 4mg

INGREDIENTS

- 1 cup white sugar
- 1 cup peanuts
- 1/2 cup light corn syrup
- 2 tablespoons butter, softened
- 1/4 teaspoon salt
- 1 teaspoon baking soda
- 1/4 cup water

DIRECTIONS

1. Grease a large cookie sheet. Set aside.
2. In a heavy 2 quart saucepan, over medium heat, bring to a boil sugar, corn syrup, salt, and water. Stir until sugar is dissolved. Stir in peanuts. Set candy thermometer in place, and continue cooking. Stir frequently until temperature reaches 300 degrees F (150 degrees C), or until a small amount of mixture dropped into very cold water separates into hard and brittle threads.
3. Remove from heat; immediately stir in butter and baking soda; pour at once onto cookie sheet. With 2 forks, lift and pull peanut mixture into rectangle about 14x12 inches; cool. Snap candy into pieces.

FRESH RHUBARB PIE

Servings: 8 | Prep: 30m | Cooks: 1h | Total: 1h30m

NUTRITION FACTS

Calories: 290 | Carbohydrates: 50.8g | Fat: 9.1g | Protein: 2.6g | Cholesterol: 4mg

INGREDIENTS

- 4 cups chopped rhubarb
- 1 tablespoon butter
- 1 1/3 cups white sugar
- 1 recipe pastry for a 9 inch double crust pie
- 6 tablespoons all-purpose flour

DIRECTIONS

1. Preheat oven to 450 degrees F (230 degrees C).
2. Combine sugar and flour. Sprinkle 1/4 of it over pastry in pie plate. Heap rhubarb over this mixture. Sprinkle with remaining sugar and flour. Dot with small pieces of butter. Cover with top crust.
3. Place pie on lowest rack in oven. Bake for 15 minutes. Reduce oven temperature to 350 degrees F (175 degrees C), and continue baking for 40 to 45 minutes. Serve warm or cold.

RHUBARB STRAWBERRY CRUNCH
Servings: 18 | Prep: 15m | Cooks: 45m | Total: 1h

NUTRITION FACTS

Calories: 253 | Carbohydrates: 38.1g | Fat: 10.8g | Protein: 2.3g | Cholesterol: 27mg

INGREDIENTS

- 1 cup white sugar
- 1 1/2 cups all-purpose flour
- 3 tablespoons all-purpose flour
- 1 cup packed brown sugar
- 3 cups sliced fresh strawberries
- 1 cup butter
- 3 cups diced rhubarb
- 1 cup rolled oats

DIRECTIONS

1. Preheat oven to 375 degrees F (190 degrees C).
2. In a large bowl, mix white sugar, 3 tablespoons flour, strawberries, and rhubarb. Place the mixture in a 9x13 inch baking dish.
3. Mix 1 1/2 cups flour, brown sugar, butter, and oats until crumbly. You may want to use a pastry blender for this. Crumble on top of the rhubarb and strawberry mixture.
4. Bake 45 minutes in the preheated oven, or until crisp and lightly browned.

STRAWBERRY CAKE FROM SCRATCH
Servings: 14 | Prep: 10m | Cooks: 30m | Total: 40m

NUTRITION FACTS

Calories: 393 | Carbohydrates: 59.3g | Fat: 15.4g | Protein: 5.4g | Cholesterol: 90mg

INGREDIENTS

- 2 cups white sugar
- 2 1/2 teaspoons baking powder
- 1 (3 ounce) package strawberry flavored Jell-O
- 1 cup whole milk, room temperature
- 1 cup butter, softened
- 1 tablespoon vanilla extract
- 4 eggs (room temperature)
- 1/2 cup strawberry puree made from frozen sweetened strawberries
- 2 3/4 cups sifted cake flour

DIRECTIONS

1. Preheat the oven to 350 degrees F (175 degrees C). Grease and flour two 9 inch round cake pans.
2. In a large bowl, cream together the butter, sugar and dry strawberry gelatin until light and fluffy. Beat in eggs one at a time, mixing well after each. Combine the flour and baking powder; stir into the batter alternately with the milk. Blend in vanilla and strawberry puree. Divide the batter evenly between the prepared pans.
3. Bake for 25 to 30 minutes in the preheated oven, or until a small knife inserted into the center of the cake comes out clean. Allow cakes to cool in their pans over a wire rack for at least 10 minutes, before tapping out to cool completely.

APPLE CRISP

Servings: 6 | Prep: 20m | Cooks: 40m | Total: 1h

NUTRITION FACTS

Calories: 361 | Carbohydrates: 55.7g | Fat: 15.6g | Protein: 2g | Cholesterol: 41mg

INGREDIENTS

- 4 cups sliced apples
- 1 cup white sugar
- 1 teaspoon ground cinnamon
- 1/2 cup butter
- 1/2 cup water
- 3/4 cup all-purpose flour

DIRECTIONS

1. Preheat oven to 350 degrees F (175 degrees C). Grease an 8x8 inch baking dish.

2. Place apples in prepared dish. Sprinkle with cinnamon. Pour water over all. In a bowl, cream together sugar and butter. Blend in flour. Sprinkle mixture evenly over apples.
3. Bake in preheated oven 30 to 40 minutes, until apples are tender and crust is golden.

MINI CHEESECAKES

Servings: 48 | Prep: 30m | Cooks: 15m | Total: 45m

NUTRITION FACTS

Calories: 95 | Carbohydrates: 11.8g | Fat: 4.8g | Protein: 1.3g | Cholesterol: 18mg

INGREDIENTS

- 1 (12 ounce) package vanilla wafers
- 2 eggs
- 2 (8 ounce) packages cream cheese
- 1 teaspoon vanilla extract
- 3/4 cup white sugar
- 1 (21 ounce) can cherry pie filling

DIRECTIONS

1. Preheat oven to 350 degrees F (175 degrees C). Line miniature muffin tins (tassie pans) with miniature paper liners.
2. Crush the vanilla wafers, and place 1/2 teaspoon of the crushed vanilla wafers into each paper cup.
3. In a mixing bowl, beat cream cheese, sugar, eggs and vanilla until light and fluffy. Fill each miniature muffin liner with this mixture, almost to the top.
4. Bake for 15 minutes. Cool. Top with a teaspoonful of cherry pie filling.

NO BAKE COOKIES

Servings: 36 | Prep: 10m | Cooks: 30m | Total: 45m | Additional: 35m

NUTRITION FACTS

Calories: 110 | Carbohydrates: 15.6g | Fat: 4.9g | Protein: 2g | Cholesterol: 7mg

INGREDIENTS

- 1 3/4 cups white sugar
- 1/2 cup crunchy peanut butter
- 1/2 cup milk
- 3 cups quick-cooking oats
- 1/2 cup butter

- 1 teaspoon vanilla extract
- 4 tablespoons unsweetened cocoa powder

DIRECTIONS

1. In a medium saucepan, combine sugar, milk, butter, and cocoa. Bring to a boil, and cook for 1 1/2 minutes. Remove from heat, and stir in peanut butter, oats, and vanilla. Drop by teaspoonfuls onto wax paper. Let cool until hardened.

MICROWAVE OVEN PEANUT BRITTLE

Servings: 16 | Prep: 10m | Cooks: 20m | Total: 30m

NUTRITION FACTS

Calories: 165 | Carbohydrates: 23.3g | Fat: 7.5g | Protein: 3.2g | Cholesterol: 2mg

INGREDIENTS

- 1 1/2 cups dry roasted peanuts
- 1 tablespoon butter
- 1 cup white sugar
- 1 teaspoon vanilla extract
- 1/2 cup light corn syrup
- 1 teaspoon baking soda
- 1 pinch salt (optional)

DIRECTIONS

1. Grease a baking sheet, and set aside. In a glass bowl, combine peanuts, sugar, corn syrup, and salt. Cook in microwave for 6 to 7 minutes on High (700 W); mixture should be bubbly and peanuts browned. Stir in butter and vanilla; cook 2 to 3 minutes longer.
2. Quickly stir in baking soda, just until mixture is foamy. Pour immediately onto greased baking sheet. Let cool 15 minutes, or until set. Break into pieces, and store in an airtight container.

APPLE CRUMBLE PIE

Servings: 8 | Prep: 30m | Cooks: 40m | Total: 1h10m

NUTRITION FACTS

Calories: 358 | Carbohydrates: 52g | Fat: 16.4g | Protein: 2.5g | Cholesterol: 23mg

INGREDIENTS

- 1 (9 inch) deep dish pie crust

- 1/3 cup white sugar
- 5 cups apples - peeled, cored and thinly sliced
- 3/4 cup all-purpose flour
- 1/2 cup white sugar
- 6 tablespoons butter
- 3/4 teaspoon ground cinnamon

DIRECTIONS

1. Preheat oven to 400 degrees F (200 degrees C.)
2. Arrange apple slices in unbaked pie shell. Mix 1/2 cup sugar and cinnamon; sprinkle over apples.
3. Mix 1/3 cup sugar with flour; cut in butter until crumbly. Spoon mixture over apples.
4. Bake in preheated oven until apples are soft and top is lightly browned, about 40 minutes.

SPANISH FLAN

Servings: 8 | Prep: 20m | Cooks: 1h | Total: 1h20m

NUTRITION FACTS

Calories: 349 | Carbohydrates: 56.7g | Fat: 9.7g | Protein: 9.5g | Cholesterol: 100mg

INGREDIENTS

- 1 cup white sugar
- 1 (12 fluid ounce) can evaporated milk
- 3 eggs
- 1 tablespoon vanilla extract
- 1 (14 ounce) can sweetened condensed milk

DIRECTIONS

1. Preheat oven to 350 degrees F (175 degrees C).
2. In a medium saucepan over medium-low heat, melt sugar until liquefied and golden in color. Carefully pour hot syrup into a 9 inch round glass baking dish, turning the dish to evenly coat the bottom and sides. Set aside.
3. In a large bowl, beat eggs. Beat in condensed milk, evaporated milk and vanilla until smooth. Pour egg mixture into baking dish. Cover with aluminum foil.
4. Bake in preheated oven 60 minutes. Let cool completely.
5. To serve, carefully invert on serving plate with edges when completely cool.

LEMON SQUARE BARS

Servings: 24 | Prep: 20m | Cooks: 50m | Total: 1h10m

Calories: 208 | Carbohydrates: 31.2g | Fat: 8.6g | Protein: 2.4g | Cholesterol: 51mg

INGREDIENTS

- 2 cups sifted all-purpose flour
- 2 cups white sugar
- 1 cup confectioners' sugar
- 1 teaspoon baking powder
- 1 cup butter, melted
- 1/4 cup all-purpose flour
- 4 eggs
- 5/8 cup lemon juice

DIRECTIONS

1. Preheat oven to 350 degrees F (175 degrees C). Grease a 9x13 inch pan.
2. In a medium bowl, stir together 2 cups flour and confectioners' sugar. Blend in the melted butter. Press into the bottom of the prepared pan.
3. Bake in the preheated oven for 15 minutes, or until golden. In a large bowl, beat eggs until light. Combine the sugar, baking powder and 1/4 cup of flour so there will be no flour lumps. Stir the sugar mixture into the eggs. Finally, stir in the lemon juice. Pour over the prepared crust and return to the oven.
4. Bake for an additional 30 minutes or until bars are set. Allow to cool completely before cutting into bars.

GINGERSNAP COOKIES

Servings: 30 | Prep: 20m | Cooks: 10m | Total: 30m

NUTRITION FACTS

Calories: 121 | Carbohydrates: 17.5g | Fat: 5.4g | Protein: 1.1g | Cholesterol: 6mg

INGREDIENTS

- 2 cups sifted all-purpose flour
- 3/4 cup shortening
- 1 tablespoon ground ginger
- 1 cup white sugar
- 2 teaspoons baking soda
- 1 egg
- 1 teaspoon ground cinnamon

- 1/4 cup dark molasses
- 1/2 teaspoon salt
- 1/3 cup cinnamon sugar

DIRECTIONS

1. Preheat oven to 350 degrees F (175 degrees C).
2. Sift the flour, ginger, baking soda, cinnamon, and salt into a mixing bowl. Stir the mixture to blend evenly, and sift a second time into another bowl.
3. Place the shortening into a mixing bowl and beat until creamy. Gradually beat in the white sugar. Beat in the egg, and dark molasses. Sift 1/3 of the flour mixture into the shortening mixture; stir to thoroughly blend. Sift in the remaining flour mixture, and mix together until a soft dough forms. Pinch off small amounts of dough and roll into 1 inch diameter balls between your hands. Roll each ball in cinnamon sugar, and place 2 inches apart on an ungreased baking sheet.
4. Bake in preheated oven until the tops are rounded and slightly cracked, about 10 minutes. Cool cookies on a wire rack. Store in an air tight container.

BROWN FAMILY'S FAVORITE PUMPKIN PIE
Servings: 8 | Prep: 30m | Cooks: 1h | Total: 1h30m

NUTRITION FACTS

Calories: 463 | Carbohydrates: 52.3g | Fat: 25.5g | Protein: 9.9g | Cholesterol: 76mg

INGREDIENTS

- 1 (15 ounce) can pumpkin puree
- 2 egg whites
- 1 (14 ounce) can sweetened condensed milk
- 1 (9 inch) unbaked pie shell
- 2 egg yolks
- 2 tablespoons all-purpose flour
- 1 teaspoon ground cinnamon
- 1/4 cup packed brown sugar
- 1/2 teaspoon ground ginger
- 1 teaspoon ground cinnamon
- 1/2 teaspoon ground nutmeg
- 2 tablespoons butter, chilled
- 1/2 teaspoon salt
- 1 cup chopped walnuts

DIRECTIONS

1. Preheat the oven to 425 degrees F (220 degrees C).

2. In a large bowl, mix together the pumpkin, sweetened condensed milk, and egg yolks. Stir in 1 teaspoon cinnamon, ginger, nutmeg, and salt. In a large glass or metal bowl, whip egg whites until soft peaks form. Gently fold into pumpkin mixture. Pour filling into pie shell.

3. Bake for 15 minutes in the preheated oven. While the pie is baking, prepare the streusel topping: In a small bowl, combine the flour, brown sugar, and 1 teaspoon cinnamon. Blend in the cold butter with a fork or pastry blender until the mixture is crumbly. Mix in the chopped nuts. Sprinkle the topping over the pie.

4. Reduce the heat to 350 degrees F (175 degrees C). Bake an additional 40 minutes, or until set.

ECLAIR CAKE

Servings: 14 | Prep: 25m | Cooks: 4h | Total: 4h25m | Additional: 4h

NUTRITION FACTS

Calories: 395 | Carbohydrates: 64.6g | Fat: 14.2g | Protein: 4.5g | Cholesterol: 4mg

INGREDIENTS

- 2 (3.5 ounce) packages instant vanilla pudding mix
- 1 (16 ounce) package graham cracker squares
- 1 (8 ounce) container frozen whipped topping, thawed
- 1 (16 ounce) package prepared chocolate frosting
- 3 cups milk

DIRECTIONS

1. Stir pudding mix, whipped topping, and milk together in a medium bowl until well blended.

2. Arrange a single layer of graham cracker squares in the bottom of a 13x9 inch baking pan. Evenly spread half of the pudding mixture over the crackers. Top with another layer of crackers and the remaining pudding mixture. Top with a final layer of graham crackers.

3. Spread the frosting over the whole cake up to the edges of the pan. Cover, and chill at least 4 hours before serving.

CREAMY PEANUT BUTTER FUDGE

Servings: 24 | Prep: 10m | Cooks: 10m | Total: 50m

NUTRITION FACTS

Calories: 357 | Carbohydrates: 54.1g | Fat: 14.6g | Protein: 5.9g | Cholesterol: 15mg

INGREDIENTS

- 4 cups white sugar
- 1 (7 ounce) jar marshmallow creme
- 1 cup light brown sugar
- 1 (16 ounce) jar peanut butter
- 1/2 cup butter
- 1 teaspoon vanilla extract
- 1 (12 fluid ounce) can evaporated milk

DIRECTIONS

1. Grease a 9x13 inch baking dish.
2. In a medium saucepan over medium heat, combine sugar, brown sugar, butter and evaporated milk. Bring to a boil, stirring constantly, and boil for 7 minutes. Remove from heat; stir in marshmallow creme until well incorporated and melted. Stir in peanut butter and vanilla until smooth; spread in prepared pan. Let cool before cutting into squares.

BANANAS FOSTER

Servings: 4 | Prep: 5m | Cooks: 15m | Total: 20m

NUTRITION FACTS

Calories: 534 | Carbohydrates: 7..2g | Fat: 23.8g | Protein: 4.6g | Cholesterol: 60mg

INGREDIENTS

- 1/4 cup butter
- 1/2 teaspoon ground cinnamon
- 2/3 cup dark brown sugar
- 3 bananas, peeled and sliced lengthwise and crosswise
- 3 1/2 tablespoons rum
- 1/4 cup coarsely chopped walnuts
- 1 1/2 teaspoons vanilla extract
- 1 pint vanilla ice cream

DIRECTIONS

1. In a large, deep skillet over medium heat, melt butter. Stir in sugar, rum, vanilla and cinnamon. When mixture begins to bubble, place bananas and walnuts in pan. Cook until bananas are hot, 1 to 2 minutes. Serve at once over vanilla ice cream.

BISCOTTI

Servings: 42 | Prep: 15m | Cooks: 25m | Total: 40m

NUTRITION FACTS

Calories: 83 | Carbohydrates: 12.3g | Fat: 3.1g | Protein: 1.4g | Cholesterol: 13mg

INGREDIENTS

- 1/2 cup vegetable oil
- 3 eggs
- 1 cup white sugar
- 1 tablespoon baking powder
- 3 1/4 cups all-purpose flour
- 1 tablespoon anise extract, or 3 drops anise oil

DIRECTIONS

1. Preheat the oven to 375 degrees F (190 degrees C). Grease cookie sheets or line with parchment paper.
2. In a medium bowl, beat together the oil, eggs, sugar and anise flavoring until well blended. Combine the flour and baking powder, stir into the egg mixture to form a heavy dough. Divide dough into two pieces. Form each piece into a roll as long as your cookie sheet. Place roll onto the prepared cookie sheet, and press down to 1/2 inch thickness.
3. Bake for 25 to 30 minutes in the preheated oven, until golden brown. Remove from the baking sheet to cool on a wire rack. When The cookies are cool enough to handle, slice each one crosswise into 1/2 inch slices. Place the slices cut side up back onto the baking sheet. Bake for an additional 6 to 10 minutes on each side. Slices should be lightly toasted.

LEMON BARS

Servings: 16 | Prep: 20m | Cooks: 50m | Total: 1h40m

NUTRITION FACTS

Calories: 153 | Carbohydrates: 21.8g | Fat: 6.7g | Protein: 1.9g | Cholesterol: 51mg

INGREDIENTS

- 1 cup all-purpose flour
- 1 large egg yolk
- 1/2 cup unsalted butter at room temperature
- 1 cup white sugar
- 1/4 cup confectioners' sugar

- 2 tablespoons all-purpose flour
- 1/4 teaspoon vanilla extract
- 1/4 cup freshly squeezed lemon juice
- 1/4 teaspoon salt
- 1 tablespoon freshly grated lemon zest
- 2 large eggs
- 1 teaspoon confectioners' sugar, or to taste

DIRECTIONS

1. Place an oven rack into middle position in oven and preheat oven to 350 degrees F (175 degrees C). Lightly oil an 8x8-inch baking dish.
2. Place 1 cup flour and butter in a mixing bowl and mash with the back of a spatula or wooden spoon until thoroughly combined. Mix in 1/4 cup confectioners' sugar, vanilla extract, and salt; mash mixture together until mixture looks like a slightly crumbly cookie dough.
3. Moisten your fingers with a little water and press dough into bottom of prepared baking dish. Use a fork to prick holes all over the crust.
4. Bake crust on center rack in the preheated oven until crust edges are barely golden brown, 22 minutes.
5. Beat eggs and egg yolks together in a bowl; whisk in white sugar and 2 tablespoons flour until smooth. Add lemon juice and lemon zest; whisk for 2 minutes. Pour lemon custard over crust.
6. Bake on center rack until custard is set and top has a thin white sugary crust, 25 minutes. Let cool completely before cutting into bars. Dip knife into very hot water, run around the edge, and cut into 16 squares. Dust cookies with 1 teaspoon confectioners' sugar.

DEEP DISH BROWNIES

Servings: 9 | Prep: 15m | Cooks: 45m | Total: 1h

NUTRITION FACTS

Calories: 340 | Carbohydrates: 44.2g | Fat: 17.8g | Protein: 4.3g | Cholesterol: 103mg

INGREDIENTS

- 3/4 cup butter, melted
- 3/4 cup all-purpose flour
- 1 1/2 cups white sugar
- 1/2 cup unsweetened cocoa powder
- 1 1/2 teaspoons vanilla extract
- 1/2 teaspoon baking powder
- 3 eggs
- 1/2 teaspoon salt

DIRECTIONS

1. Preheat oven to 350 degrees F (175 degrees C). Grease an 8 inch square pan.
2. In a large bowl, blend melted butter, sugar and vanilla. Beat in eggs one at a time. Combine the flour, cocoa, baking powder and salt. Gradually blend into the egg mixture. Spread the batter into the prepared pan.
3. Bake in preheated oven for 40 to 45 minutes, or until brownies begin to pull away from the sides of the pan. Let brownies cool, then cut into squares. Enjoy!

BEST EVER BLUEBERRY COBBLER

Servings: 6 | Prep: 20m | Cooks: 40m | Total: 1h

NUTRITION FACTS

Calories: 335 | Carbohydrates: 45.6g | Fat: 16.6g | Protein: 3.3g | Cholesterol: 72mg

INGREDIENTS

- 3 cups fresh blueberries
- 1 pinch salt
- 3 tablespoons white sugar
- 1/2 cup butter, softened
- 1/3 cup orange juice
- 1/2 cup white sugar
- 2/3 cup all-purpose flour
- 1 egg
- 1/4 teaspoon baking powder
- 1/2 teaspoon vanilla extract

DIRECTIONS

1. Preheat oven to 375 degrees F (190 degrees C).
2. In an 8 inch square baking dish, mix blueberries, 3 tablespoons sugar, and orange juice. Set aside. In a small bowl, thoroughly mix flour, baking powder, and salt. Set aside.
3. In a medium bowl, cream butter and 1/2 cup sugar until light and fluffy. Beat in egg and vanilla extract. Gradually add flour mixture, stirring just until ingredients are combined. Drop batter by rounded tablespoons over blueberry mixture. Try to cover as much of filling as possible.
4. Bake in preheated oven for 35 to 40 minutes, until topping is golden brown and filling is bubbling.

BLACKBERRY COBBLER

Servings: 8 | Prep: 20m | Cooks: 25m | Total: 45m

NUTRITION FACTS

Calories: 318 | Carbohydrates: 58.4g | Fat: 9.1g | Protein: 2.7g | Cholesterol: 23mg

INGREDIENTS

- 1 cup all-purpose flour
- 1/4 cup boiling water
- 1 1/2 cups white sugar, divided
- 2 tablespoons cornstarch
- 1 teaspoon baking powder
- 1/4 cup cold water
- 1/2 teaspoon salt
- 1 tablespoon lemon juice
- 6 tablespoons cold butter
- 4 cups fresh blackberries, rinsed and drained

DIRECTIONS

1. Preheat oven to 400 degrees F (200 degrees C). Line a baking sheet with aluminum foil.
2. In a large bowl, mix the flour, 1/2 cup sugar, baking powder, and salt. Cut in butter until the mixture resembles coarse crumbs. Stir in 1/4 cup boiling water just until mixture is evenly moist.
3. In a separate bowl, dissolve the cornstarch in cold water. Mix in remaining 1 cup sugar, lemon juice, and blackberries. Transfer to a cast iron skillet, and bring to a boil, stirring frequently. Drop dough into the skillet by spoonfuls. Place skillet on the foil lined baking sheet.
4. Bake 25 minutes in the preheated oven, until dough is golden brown.

WHITE CHOCOLATE MACADAMIA NUT COOKIES
Servings: 48 | Prep: 15m | Cooks: 10m | Total: 45m | Additional: 20m

NUTRITION FACTS

Calories: 122 | Carbohydrates: 13g | Fat: 7.4g | Protein: 1.4g | Cholesterol: 19mg

INGREDIENTS

- 1 cup butter, softened
- 2 1/2 cups all-purpose flour
- 3/4 cup packed light brown sugar
- 1 teaspoon baking soda
- 1/2 cup white sugar
- 1/2 teaspoon salt
- 2 eggs
- 1 cup coarsely chopped macadamia nuts
- 1/2 teaspoon vanilla extract
- 1 cup coarsely chopped white chocolate
- 1/2 teaspoon almond extract

1. Preheat oven to 350 degrees F (175 degrees C).
2. In a large bowl, cream together the butter, brown sugar, and white sugar until smooth. Beat in the eggs, one at a time, then stir in the vanilla and almond extracts. Combine the flour, baking soda, and salt; gradually stir into the creamed mixture. Mix in the macadamia nuts and white chocolate. Drop dough by teaspoonfuls onto ungreased cookie sheets.
3. Bake for 10 minutes in the preheated oven, or until golden brown.

CHOCOLATE LOVERS' FAVORITE CAKE

Servings: 12 | Prep: 30m | Cooks: 1h | Total: 2h | Additional: 30m

NUTRITION FACTS

Calories: 604 | Carbohydrates: 57.7g | Fat: 40g | Protein: 8.8g | Cholesterol: 144mg

INGREDIENTS

- 1 (18.25 ounce) package devil's food cake mix
- 5 eggs
- 1 (3.9 ounce) package instant chocolate pudding mix
- 1 teaspoon almond extract
- 2 cups sour cream
- 2 cups semisweet chocolate chips
- 1 cup melted butter

DIRECTIONS

1. Preheat oven to 350 degrees F (175 degrees C). Grease a 10 inch Bundt pan.
2. In a large bowl, stir together cake mix and pudding mix. Make a well in the center and pour in sour cream, melted butter, eggs and almond extract. Beat on low speed until blended. Scrape bowl, and beat 4 minutes on medium speed. Blend in chocolate chips. Pour batter into prepared pan.
3. ake in preheated oven for 50 to 55 minutes. Let cool in pan for 10 minutes, then turn out onto a wire rack and cool completely.

GINGERBREAD MEN

Servings: 30 | Prep: 25m | Cooks: 12m | Total: 1h37m | Additional: 1h

NUTRITION FACTS

Calories: 79 | Carbohydrates: 11.5g | Fat: 3.3g | Protein: 1g | Cholesterol: 14mg

INGREDIENTS

- 1 (3.5 ounce) package cook and serve butterscotch pudding mix
- 1 1/2 cups all-purpose flour
- 1/2 cup butter
- 1/2 teaspoon baking soda
- 1/2 cup packed brown sugar
- 1 1/2 teaspoons ground ginger
- 1 egg
- 1 teaspoon ground cinnamon

DIRECTIONS

1. In a medium bowl, cream together the dry butterscotch pudding mix, butter, and brown sugar until smooth. Stir in the egg. Combine the flour, baking soda, ginger, and cinnamon; stir into the pudding mixture. Cover, and chill dough until firm, about 1 hour.
2. Preheat the oven to 350 degrees F (175 degrees C). Grease baking sheets. On a floured board, roll dough out to about 1/8 inch thickness, and cut into man shapes using a cookie cutter. Place cookies 2 inches apart on the prepared baking sheets.
3. Bake for 10 to 12 minutes in the preheated oven, until cookies are golden at the edges. Cool on wire racks.

COCONUT POKE CAKE

Servings: 24 | Prep: 30m | Cooks: 1h | Total: 2h | Additional: 30m

NUTRITION FACTS

Calories: 304 | Carbohydrates: 43.4g | Fat: 13.8g | Protein: 3g | Cholesterol: 6mg

INGREDIENTS

- 1 (18.25 ounce) package white cake mix
- 1 (16 ounce) package frozen whipped topping, thawed
- 1 (14 ounce) can cream of coconut
- 1 (8 ounce) package flaked coconut
- 1 (14 ounce) can sweetened condensed milk

DIRECTIONS

1. Prepare and bake white cake mix according to package directions. Remove cake from oven. While still hot, using a utility fork, poke holes all over the top of the cake.

2. Mix cream of coconut and sweetened condensed milk together. Pour over the top of the still hot cake. Let cake cool completely then frost with the whipped topping and top with the flaked coconut. Keep cake refrigerated.

PUPPY CHOW

Servings: 36 | Prep: 5m | Cooks: 5m | Total: 10m

NUTRITION FACTS

Calories: 90 | Carbohydrates: 14.7g | Fat: 3.2g | Protein: 1.7g | Cholesterol: 0mg

INGREDIENTS

- 9 cups crispy rice cereal squares
- 1 cup semi-sweet chocolate chips
- 1/2 cup peanut butter
- 1 1/2 cups confectioners' sugar

DIRECTIONS

1. In a saucepan over low heat, melt the chocolate; add peanut butter and mix until smooth.
2. Remove from heat, add cereal and stir until coated.
3. Pour powdered sugar into large plastic bag, add coated cereal and shake until well coated. Store in airtight container.

PUMPKIN CAKE

Servings: 14 | Prep: 30m | Cooks: 30m | Total: 1h

NUTRITION FACTS

Calories: 438 | Carbohydrates: 46.8g | Fat: 26.8g | Protein: 5.3g | Cholesterol: 53mg

INGREDIENTS

- 2 cups white sugar
- 3 teaspoons baking powder
- 1 1/4 cups vegetable oil
- 2 teaspoons baking soda
- 1 teaspoon vanilla extract
- 1/4 teaspoon salt
- 2 cups canned pumpkin
- 2 teaspoons ground cinnamon
- 4 eggs

- 1 cup chopped walnuts (optional)
- 2 cups all-purpose flour

DIRECTIONS

1. Preheat oven to 350 degrees F (175 degrees C). Grease and flour a 12x18 inch pan. Sift together the flour, baking powder, baking soda, salt and cinnamon. Set aside.
2. In a large bowl combine sugar and oil. Blend in vanilla and pumpkin, then beat in eggs one at a time. Gradually beat in flour mixture. Stir in nuts. Spread batter into prepared 12x18 inch pan.
3. Bake in the preheated oven for 30 minutes, or until a toothpick inserted into the center of the cake comes out clean. Allow to cool.

PEACH COBBLER DUMP CAKE

Servings: 24 | Prep: 10m | Cooks: 45m | Total: 55m

NUTRITION FACTS

Calories: 155 | Carbohydrates: 24.3g | Fat: 6.4g | Protein: 1.2g | Cholesterol: 11mg

INGREDIENTS

- 2 (16 ounce) cans peaches in heavy syrup
- 1/2 cup butter
- 1 (18.25 ounce) package yellow cake mix
- 1/2 teaspoon ground cinnamon, or to taste

DIRECTIONS

1. Preheat oven to 375 degrees F (190 degrees C).
2. Empty peaches into the bottom of one 9x13 inch pan. Cover with the dry cake mix and press down firmly. Cut butter into small pieces and place on top of cake mix. Sprinkle top with cinnamon.
3. Bake at 375 degrees F (190 degrees C) for 45 minutes.

APPLE OATMEAL CRISP

Servings: 8 | Prep: 20m | Cooks: 40m | Total: 1h

NUTRITION FACTS

Calories: 376 | Carbohydrates: 65.2g | Fat: 12.4g | Protein: 3.2g | Cholesterol: 31mg

INGREDIENTS

- 1 cup brown sugar

- 3 cups apples - peeled, cored and chopped
- 1 cup rolled oats
- 1/2 cup white sugar
- 1 cup all-purpose flour
- 2 teaspoons ground cinnamon
- 1/2 cup butter, melted

DIRECTIONS

1. Preheat oven to 350 degrees F (175 degrees C). Lightly grease an 8-inch square pan.
2. In a large bowl, combine brown sugar, oats, flour and butter. Mix until crumbly. Place half of crumb mixture in pan. Spread the apples evenly over crumb mixture. Sprinkle with sugar and cinnamon and top with remaining crumb mixture.
3. Bake in the preheated oven for 40 to 45 minutes, or until golden brown.

CHEWY PEANUT BUTTER BROWNIES

Servings: 16 | Prep: 15m | Cooks: 25m | Total: 40m

NUTRITION FACTS

Calories: 177 | Carbohydrates: 22.8g | Fat: 8.5g | Protein: 3.7g | Cholesterol: 23mg

INGREDIENTS

- 1/2 cup peanut butter
- 1/2 teaspoon vanilla extract
- 1/3 cup margarine, softened
- 1 cup all-purpose flour
- 2/3 cup white sugar
- 1 teaspoon baking powder
- 1/2 cup packed brown sugar
- 1/4 teaspoon salt
- 2 egg

DIRECTIONS

1. Stir the honey, orange zest, garlic, soy sauce, balsamic vinegar, pepper, and water together in a bowl. Add the green beans and toss to coat. Allow to soak for 20 minutes, mixing every 5 minutes.
2. Heat the olive oil in a saucepan over low heat; add the green beans to the hot oil and cover the saucepan. Pour the green beans and sauce into the pan and cook, shaking the pan regularly, until the beans are slightly tender, about 5 minutes.
3. Bake for 30 to 35 minutes in preheated oven, or until the top springs back when touched. Cool, and cut into 16 squares.

AUTUMN CHEESECAKE

Servings: 12 | Prep: 30m | Cooks: 1h10m | Total: 4h | Additional: 2h20

NUTRITION FACTS

Calories: 341 | Carbohydrates: 30.3g | Fat: 23.4g | Protein: 5.1g | Cholesterol: 82mg

INGREDIENTS

- 1 cup graham cracker crumbs
- 2 eggs
- 1/2 cup finely chopped pecans
- 1/2 teaspoon vanilla extract
- 3 tablespoons white sugar
- 4 cups apples - peeled, cored and thinly sliced
- 1/2 teaspoon ground cinnamon
- 1/3 cup white sugar
- 1/4 cup unsalted butter, melted
- 1/2 teaspoon ground cinnamon
- 2 (8 ounce) packages cream cheese, softened
- 1/4 cup chopped pecans
- 1/2 cup white sugar

DIRECTIONS

1. Preheat oven to 350 degrees F (175 degrees C). In a large bowl, stir together the graham cracker crumbs, 1/2 cup finely chopped pecans, 3 tablespoons sugar, 1/2 teaspoon cinnamon and melted butter; press into the bottom of a 9 inch springform pan. Bake in preheated oven for 10 minutes.
2. In a large bowl, combine cream cheese and 1/2 cup sugar. Mix at medium speed until smooth. Beat in eggs one at a time, mixing well after each addition. Blend in vanilla; pour filling into the baked crust.
3. In a small bowl, stir together 1/3 cup sugar and 1/2 teaspoon cinnamon. Toss the cinnamon-sugar with the apples to coat. Spoon apple mixture over cream cheese layer and sprinkle with 1/4 cup chopped pecans.
4. Bake in preheated oven for 60 to 70 minutes. With a knife, loosen cake from rim of pan. Let cool, then remove the rim of pan. Chill cake before serving.

FROSTED BANANA BARS

Servings: 36 | Prep: 20m | Cooks: 20m | Total: 40m

NUTRITION FACTS

Calories: 160 | Carbohydrates: 22.9g | Fat: 7.3g | Protein: 1.4g | Cholesterol: 20mg

INGREDIENTS

- 1/2 cup butter, softened
- 2 cups all-purpose flour
- 1 1/2 cups white sugar
- 1 teaspoon baking soda
- 2 eggs
- 1/4 teaspoon salt
- 1 cup sour cream
- 1 cup mashed ripe bananas
- 1 teaspoon vanilla extract
- 1 (16 ounce) container cream cheese frosting

DIRECTIONS

1. Preheat oven to 350 degrees F (175 degrees C). Grease a 10x15 inch jellyroll pan.
2. In a large bowl, cream together the butter and sugar until smooth. Beat in the eggs, one at a time, then stir in the sour cream and vanilla. Combine the flour, baking soda and salt; stir into the batter. Finally, mix in the mashed banana. Spread evenly into the prepared pan.
3. Bake for 20 to 25 minutes in the preheated oven, until a toothpick inserted into the center comes out clean. Allow bars to cool completely before frosting with the cream cheese frosting.

HASTY CHOCOLATE PUDDING

Servings: 4 | Prep: 5m | Cooks: 10m | Total: 15m

NUTRITION FACTS

Calories: 203 | Carbohydrates: 40.3g | Fat: 3.4g | Protein: 5.4g | Cholesterol: 10mg

INGREDIENTS

- 1/2 cup white sugar
- 2 cups milk
- 1/3 cup unsweetened cocoa powder
- 2 teaspoons vanilla extract
- 3 tablespoons cornstarch

DIRECTIONS

1. In a microwave-safe bowl, whisk together the sugar, cocoa and cornstarch. Whisk in milk a little at a time so the mixture does not have any dry lumps.

2. Place in the microwave, and cook for 3 minutes on high. Stir, then cook at 1 minute intervals, stirring between cooking times for 2 to 4 minutes, or until shiny and thick. Stir in vanilla.

3. Place a piece of plastic wrap directly on the surface of the pudding to prevent a skin from forming, and chill in the refrigerator. Serve cold.

ONE BOWL BROWNIES

Servings: 12 | Prep: 10m | Cooks: 35m | Total: 45m

NUTRITION FACTS

Calories: 398 | Carbohydrates: 45.5g | Fat: 24.1g | Protein: 5.5g | Cholesterol: 77mg

INGREDIENTS

- 4 (1 ounce) squares unsweetened chocolate, chopped
- 1 teaspoon vanilla extract
- 3/4 cup butter
- 1 cup all-purpose flour
- 2 cups white sugar
- 1 cup chopped walnuts
- 3 eggs

DIRECTIONS

1. Preheat oven to 350 degrees F (180 degrees C). Grease a 13x9-inch pan.
2. Microwave chocolate and butter in large bowl at HIGH for 2 minutes or until butter is melted. Alternately, melt butter and chocolate in a double boiler over simmering water.
3. Remove bowl from microwave and stir until chocolate is melted. Stir in sugar. Mix in eggs and vanilla. Stir in flour and nuts.
4. Spread batter into prepared pan. Bake for 35 minutes (do not overbake).

PUMPKIN GINGER CUPCAKES

Servings: 24 | Prep: 20m | Cooks: 20m | Total: 1h30m | Additional: 50m

NUTRITION FACTS

Calories: 211 | Carbohydrates: 31.8g | Fat: 8.7g | Protein: 2.4g | Cholesterol: 51mg

INGREDIENTS

- 2 cups all-purpose flour
- 1/3 cup finely chopped crystallized ginger
- 1 (3.4 ounce) package instant butterscotch pudding mix

- 1 cup butter, room temperature
- 2 teaspoons baking soda
- 1 cup white sugar
- 1/4 teaspoon salt
- 1 cup packed brown sugar
- 1 tablespoon ground cinnamon
- 4 eggs, room temperature
- 1/2 teaspoon ground ginger
- 1 teaspoon vanilla extract
- 1/2 teaspoon ground allspice
- 1 (15 ounce) can pumpkin puree
- 1/4 teaspoon ground cloves

DIRECTIONS

1. Preheat an oven to 350 degrees F (175 degrees C). Grease 24 muffin cups, or line with paper muffin liners. Whisk together the flour, pudding mix, baking soda, salt, cinnamon, ground ginger, allspice, cloves, and crystallized ginger in a bowl; set aside.
2. Beat the butter, white sugar, and brown sugar with an electric mixer in a large bowl until light and fluffy. The mixture should be noticeably lighter in color. Add the eggs one at a time, allowing each egg to blend into the butter mixture before adding the next. Beat in the vanilla and pumpkin puree with the last egg. Stir in the flour mixture, mixing until just incorporated. Pour the batter into the prepared muffin cups.
3. Bake in the preheated oven until golden and the tops spring back when lightly pressed, about 20 minutes. Cool in the pans for 10 minutes before removing to cool completely on a wire rack.

COFFEE CAKE

Servings: 15 | Prep: 20m | Cooks: 25m | Total: 45m

NUTRITION FACTS

Calories: 235 | Carbohydrates: 34.1g | Fat: 10g | Protein: 2.9g | Cholesterol: 38mg

INGREDIENTS

- 2 cups all-purpose flour
- 3/4 cup milk, or as needed
- 3/4 cup white sugar
- 1 1/2 teaspoons vanilla extract
- 2 teaspoons baking powder
- 1/4 cup all-purpose flour

- 1/2 teaspoon salt
- 2/3 cup white sugar
- 1/2 cup butter
- 1 teaspoon ground cinnamon
- 1 egg
- 1/4 cup butter

DIRECTIONS

1. Preheat oven to 350 degrees F (175 degrees C). Grease and flour a 9x13 inch pan. Make the streusel topping: In a medium bowl, combine 1/4 cup flour, 2/3 cup sugar and 1 teaspoon cinnamon. Cut in 1/4 cup butter until mixture resembles coarse crumbs. Set aside.
2. In a large bowl, combine 2 cups flour, 3/4 cup sugar, baking powder and salt. Cut in 1/2 cup butter until mixture resembles coarse crumbs. Crack an egg into a measuring cup and then fill add milk to make 1 cup. Stir in vanilla. Pour into crumb mixture and mix just until moistened. Spread into prepared pan. Sprinkle top with streusel.
3. Bake in the preheated oven for 25 to 30 minutes, or until a toothpick inserted into the center of the cake comes out clean. Allow to cool.

SNICKERDOODLES

Servings: 36 | Prep: 15m | Cooks: 10m | Total: 30m | Additional: 5m

NUTRITION FACTS

Calories: 125 | Carbohydrates: 16.5g | Fat: 6.1g | Protein: 1.3g | Cholesterol: 10mg

INGREDIENTS

- 1 cup shortening
- 2 teaspoons cream of tartar
- 1 1/2 cups white sugar
- 1/2 teaspoon salt
- 2 eggs
- 2 tablespoons white sugar
- 2 3/4 cups all-purpose flour
- 2 teaspoons ground cinnamon
- 1 teaspoon baking soda

DIRECTIONS

1. Preheat oven to 375 degrees F (190 degrees C).

2. In a medium bowl, cream together the shortening and 1 1/2 cups sugar. Stir in the eggs. Sift together the flour, baking soda, cream of tartar, and salt; stir into the creamed mixture until well blended. In a small bowl, stir together the 2 tablespoons of sugar, and the cinnamon. Roll dough into walnut sized balls, then roll the balls in the cinnamon-sugar. Place them onto an unprepared cookie sheet, two inches apart.

3. Bake for 8 to 10 minutes in the preheated oven. Edges should be slightly brown. Remove from sheets to cool on wire racks.

CHOCOLATE ZUCCHINI CAKE

Servings: 24 | Prep: 15m | Cooks: 50m | Total: 1h5m

NUTRITION FACTS

Calories: 269 | Carbohydrates: 27.2g | Fat: 1.3g | Protein: 3.4g | Cholesterol: 31mg

INGREDIENTS

- 2 cups all-purpose flour
- 1 teaspoon ground cinnamon
- 2 cups white sugar
- 4 eggs
- 3/4 cup unsweetened cocoa powder
- 1 1/2 cups vegetable oil
- 2 teaspoons baking soda
- 3 cups grated zucchini
- 1 teaspoon baking powder
- 3/4 cup chopped walnuts
- 1/2 teaspoon salt

DIRECTIONS

1. Preheat oven to 350 degrees F (175 degrees C). Grease and flour a 9x13 inch baking pan.

2. In a medium bowl, stir together the flour, sugar, cocoa, baking soda, baking powder, salt and cinnamon. Add the eggs and oil, mix well. Fold in the nuts and zucchini until they are evenly distributed. Pour into the prepared pan.

3. Bake for 50 to 60 minutes in the preheated oven, until a knife inserted into the center comes out clean. Cool cake completely before frosting with your favorite frosting.

APPLE CRUMB PIE

Servings: 8 | Prep: 30m | Cooks: 50m | Total: 3h20m | Additional: 2h

Calories: 408 | Carbohydrates: 69.9g | Fat: 14.6g | Protein: 3.5g | Cholesterol: 11mg

INGREDIENTS

- 1 (9 inch) pie shell
- 1/8 teaspoon ground nutmeg
- 6 cups thinly sliced apples
- 1/2 cup raisins (optional)
- 1 tablespoon lemon juice (optional)
- 1/2 cup chopped walnuts (optional)
- 3/4 cup white sugar
- 1/2 cup all-purpose flour
- 2 tablespoons all-purpose flour
- 1/2 cup packed brown sugar
- 1/2 teaspoon ground cinnamon
- 3 tablespoons butter

DIRECTIONS

1. Preheat oven to 375 degrees F (190 degrees C).
2. Place sliced apples in a large bowl; sprinkle with lemon juice, if desired. In a small bowl, mix together white sugar, 2 tablespoons flour, cinnamon, and nutmeg. Sprinkle mixture over apples and toss until apple slices are evenly coated. Stir in raisins and walnuts (optional). Transfer mixture into pastry shell.
3. In a small bowl ,mix together 1/2 cup flour and brown sugar. Cut in butter or margarine until mixture is crumbly. Sprinkle mixture over apple filling. Cover top loosely with aluminum foil.
4. Bake in preheated oven for 25 minutes. Remove foil and bake an additional 25 to 30 minutes, until top is golden brown and filling is bubbly. Cool on a wire rack.

PINEAPPLE UPSIDE-DOWN CAKE

Servings: 12 | Prep: 20m | Cooks: 45m | Total: 1h5m

NUTRITION FACTS

Calories: 360 | Carbohydrates: 61.8g | Fat: 12.3g | Protein: 2g | Cholesterol: 20mg

INGREDIENTS

- 1/2 cup butter
- 10 maraschino cherries
- 1 1/2 cups brown sugar

- 1 (18.25 ounce) package white cake mix
- 1 (20 ounce) can sliced pineapple

DIRECTIONS

1. Melt the butter over medium high heat in the iron skillet. Remove from the heat and sprinkle the brown sugar evenly to cover the butter. Next, arrange pineapple rings around the bottom of the pan, one layer deep. Place a maraschino cherry into the center of each pineapple ring. Prepare the cake mix as directed by the manufacturer, substitute some of the pineapple juice for some of the liquid in the directions. Pour the batter over the pineapple layer.
2. Bake as directed by the cake mix directions. Cool for 10 minutes, then carefully turn out onto a plate. Do not let the cake cool too much or it will be stuck to the pan.

VEGAN CHOCOLATE CAKE
Servings: 8 | Prep: 15m | Cooks: 45m | Total: 1h

NUTRITION FACTS

Calories: 275 | Carbohydrates: 44.6g | Fat: 9.7g | Protein: 3g | Cholesterol: 0mg

INGREDIENTS

- 1 1/2 cups all-purpose flour
- 1/3 cup vegetable oil
- 1 cup white sugar
- 1 teaspoon vanilla extract
- 1/4 cup cocoa powder
- 1 teaspoon distilled white vinegar
- 1 teaspoon baking soda
- 1 cup water
- 1/2 teaspoon salt

DIRECTIONS

1. Preheat oven to 350 degrees F (175 degrees C). Lightly grease one 9x5 inch loaf pan.
2. Sift together the flour, sugar, cocoa, baking soda and salt. Add the oil, vanilla, vinegar and water. Mix together until smooth.
3. Pour into prepared pan and bake at 350 degrees F (175 degrees C) for 45 minutes. Remove from oven and allow to cool.

BANANA CAKE

Servings: 12 | Prep: 30m | Cooks: 30m | Total: 1h

NUTRITION FACTS

Calories: 346 | Carbohydrates: 55.8g | Fat: 12.2g | Protein: 5.5g | Cholesterol: 52mg

INGREDIENTS

- 2 1/2 cups all-purpose flour
- 3/4 cup light brown sugar
- 1 tablespoon baking soda
- 2 eggs
- 1 pinch salt
- 4 ripe bananas, mashed
- 1/2 cup unsalted butter
- 2/3 cup buttermilk
- 1 cup white sugar
- 1/2 cup chopped walnuts

DIRECTIONS

1. Preheat oven to 350 degrees F (175 degrees C). Grease and flour 2 - 8 inch round pans. In a small bowl, whisk together flour, baking soda and salt; set aside.
2. In a large bowl, cream butter, white sugar and brown sugar until light and fluffy. Beat in eggs, one at a time. Mix in the bananas. Add flour mixture alternately with the buttermilk to the creamed mixture. Stir in chopped walnuts. Pour batter into the prepared pans.
3. Bake in the preheated oven for 30 minutes. Remove from oven, and place on a damp tea towel to cool.

APPLE CRISP WITH OAT TOPPING

Servings: 4 | Prep: 20m | Cooks: 40m | Total: 1h

NUTRITION FACTS

Calories: 618 | Carbohydrates: 99.3g | Fat: 24.6g | Protein: 5.3g | Cholesterol: 61mg

INGREDIENTS

- 6 apples - peeled, cored, and sliced
- 3/4 cup old-fashioned oats
- 2 tablespoons white sugar
- 3/4 cup all-purpose flour

- 1/2 teaspoon ground cinnamon
- 1 teaspoon ground cinnamon
- 1 cup brown sugar
- 1/2 cup cold butter

DIRECTIONS

1. Preheat oven to 350 degrees F (175 degrees C).
2. Toss apples with white sugar and 1/2 teaspoon cinnamon in a medium bowl to coat; pour into a 9-inch square baking dish.
3. Mix brown sugar, oats, flour, and 1 teaspoon cinnamon in a separate bowl. Use a pastry cutter or 2 forks to mash cold butter into the oats mixture until the mixture resembles coarse crumbs; spread over the apples to the edges of the baking dish. Pat the topping gently until even.
4. Bake in preheated oven until golden brown and sides are bubbling, about 40 minutes.

CARAMEL SHORTBREAD SQUARES

Servings: 40 | Prep: 10m | Cooks: 25m | Total: 35m

NUTRITION FACTS

Calories: 119 | Carbohydrates: 13.2g | Fat: 7.3g | Protein: 1.1g | Cholesterol: 17mg

INGREDIENTS

- 2/3 cup butter, softened
- 1/4 cup white sugar
- 1 1/4 cups all-purpose flour
- 1/2 cup butter
- 1/2 cup packed light brown sugar
- 2 tablespoons light corn syrup
- 1/2 cup sweetened condensed milk
- 1 1/4 cups milk chocolate chips

DIRECTIONS

1. Preheat oven to 350 degrees F (175 C).
2. In a medium bowl, mix together 2/3 cup butter, white sugar, and flour until evenly crumbly. Press into a 9 inch square baking pan. Bake for 20 minutes.
3. In a 2 quart saucepan, combine 1/2 cup butter, brown sugar, corn syrup, and sweetened condensed milk. Bring to a boil. Continue to boil for 5 minutes. Remove from heat and beat vigorously with a wooden spoon for about 3 minutes. Pour over baked crust (warm or cool). Cool until it begins to firm.
4. Place chocolate in a microwave-safe bowl. Heat for 1 minute, then stir and continue to heat and stir at 20 second intervals until chocolate is melted and smooth. Pour chocolate over the caramel layer

and spread evenly to cover completely. Chill. Cut into 1 inch squares. These need to be small because they are so rich.

GARBANZO BEAN CHOCOLATE CAKE

Servings: 12 | Prep: 15m | Cooks: 40m | Total: 1h10m | Additional: 15m

NUTRITION FACTS

Calories: 229 | Carbohydrates: 36.8g | Fat: 8.5g | Protein: 5.2g | Cholesterol: 62mg

INGREDIENTS

- 1 1/2 cups semisweet chocolate chips
- 3/4 cup white sugar
- 1 (19 ounce) can garbanzo beans, rinsed and drained
- 1/2 teaspoon baking powder
- 4 eggs
- 1 tablespoon confectioners' sugar for dusting

DIRECTIONS

1. Preheat the oven to 350 degrees F (175 degrees C). Grease a 9-inch round cake pan.
2. Place the chocolate chips into a microwave-safe bowl. Cook in the microwave for about 2 minutes, stirring every 20 seconds after the first minute, until chocolate is melted and smooth. If you have a powerful microwave, reduce the power to 50 percent.
3. Combine the beans and eggs in the bowl of a food processor. Process until smooth. Add the sugar and the baking powder, and pulse to blend. Pour in the melted chocolate and blend until smooth, scraping down the corners to make sure chocolate is completely mixed. Transfer the batter to the prepared cake pan.
4. Bake for 40 minutes in the preheated oven, or until a knife inserted into the center of the cake comes out clean. Cool in the pan on a wire rack for 10 to 15 minutes before inverting onto a serving plate. Dust with confectioners' sugar just before serving.

CAKE MIX COOKIES

Servings: 24 | Prep: 10m | Cooks: 8m | Total: 25m | Additional: 7m

NUTRITION FACTS

Calories: 166 | Carbohydrates: 20.2g | Fat: 9.7g | Protein: 2.1g | Cholesterol: 26mg

INGREDIENTS

- 1 (18.25 ounce) package chocolate cake mix
- 2 eggs
- 1/2 cup butter, softened
- 1 cup semisweet chocolate chips

DIRECTIONS

1. Preheat oven to 350 degrees F (175 degrees C).
2. In a medium bowl, stir together the cake mix, butter and eggs until smooth and well blended. Mix in the chocolate chips. Drop by spoonfuls onto ungreased baking sheets.
3. Bake for 8 to 10 minutes in the preheated oven. Allow cookies to cool on baking sheet for 5 minutes before removing to a wire rack to cool completely.

GERMAN CHOCOLATE CAKE

Servings: 12 | Prep: 30m | Cooks: 30m | Total: 1h

NUTRITION FACTS

Calories: 735 | Carbohydrates: 88.3g | Fat: 40.6g | Protein: 9.1g | Cholesterol: 187mg

INGREDIENTS

- 1/2 cup water
- 4 egg whites
- 4 (1 ounce) squares German sweet chocolate
- 1 cup white sugar
- 1 cup butter, softened
- 1 cup evaporated milk
- 2 cups white sugar
- 1/2 cup butter
- 4 egg yolks
- 3 egg yolks, beaten
- 1 teaspoon vanilla extract
- 1 1/3 cups flaked coconut
- 1 cup buttermilk
- 1 cup chopped pecans
- 2 1/2 cups cake flour
- 1 teaspoon vanilla extract
- 1 teaspoon baking soda
- 1/2 teaspoon shortening
- 1/2 teaspoon salt
- 1 (1 ounce) square semisweet chocolate

DIRECTIONS

1. Preheat oven to 350 degrees F (175 degrees C). Grease and flour 3 - 9 inch round pans. Sift together the flour, baking soda and salt. Set aside. In a small saucepan, heat water and 4 ounces chocolate until melted. Remove from heat and allow to cool.

2. In a large bowl, cream 1 cup butter and 2 cups sugar until light and fluffy. Beat in 4 egg yolks one at a time. Blend in the melted chocolate mixture and vanilla. Beat in the flour mixture alternately with the buttermilk, mixing just until incorporated.

3. In a large glass or metal mixing bowl, beat egg whites until stiff peaks form. Fold 1/3 of the whites into the batter, then quickly fold in remaining whites until no streaks remain.

4. Pour into 3 - 9 inch pans Bake in the preheated oven for 30 minutes, or until a toothpick inserted into the center of the cake comes out clean. Allow to cool for 10 minutes in the pan, then turn out onto wire rack.

5. To make the Filling: In a saucepan combine 1 cup sugar, evaporated milk, 1/2 cup butter, and 3 egg yolks. Cook over low heat, stirring constantly until thickened. Remove from heat. Stir in coconut, pecans and vanilla. Cool until thick enough to spread.

6. Spread filling between layers and on top of cake. In a small saucepan, melt shortening and 1 ounce of chocolate. Stir until smooth and drizzle down the sides of the cake.

BLACK BEAN BROWNIES
Servings: 16 | Prep: 10m | Cooks: 30m | Total: 40m

NUTRITION FACTS

Calories: 126 | Carbohydrates: 18.1g | Fat: 5.3g | Protein: 3.3g | Cholesterol: 35mg

INGREDIENTS

- 1 (15.5 ounce) can black beans, rinsed and drained
- 1 teaspoon vanilla extract
- 3 eggs
- 3/4 cup white sugar
- 3 tablespoons vegetable oil
- 1 teaspoon instant coffee (optional)
- 1/4 cup cocoa powder
- 1/2 cup milk chocolate chips (optional)
- 1 pinch salt

DIRECTIONS

1. Preheat oven to 350 degrees F (175 degrees C). Lightly grease an 8x8 square baking dish.

2. Combine the black beans, eggs, oil, cocoa powder, salt, vanilla extract, sugar, and instant coffee in a blender; blend until smooth; pour the mixture into the prepared baking dish. Sprinkle the chocolate chips over the top of the mixture.

3. Bake in the preheated oven until the top is dry and the edges start to pull away from the sides of the pan, about 30 minutes.

ORANGE CAKE

Servings: 12 | Prep: 30m | Cooks: 1h | Total: 2h | Additional: 30m

NUTRITION FACTS

Calories: 410 | Carbohydrates: 55g | Fat: 19.8g | Protein: 4.2g | Cholesterol: 73mg

INGREDIENTS

- 1 (18.25 ounce) package yellow cake mix
- 1 teaspoon lemon extract
- 1 (3 ounce) package instant lemon pudding mix
- 1/3 cup orange juice
- 3/4 cup orange juice
- 2/3 cup white sugar
- 1/2 cup vegetable oil
- 1/4 cup butter
- 4 eggs

DIRECTIONS

1. Grease a 10 inch Bundt pan. Preheat oven to 325 degrees F (165 degrees C).

2. In a large bowl, stir together cake mix and pudding mix. Make a well in the center and pour in 3/4 cup orange juice, oil, eggs and lemon extract. Beat on low speed until blended. Scrape bowl, and beat 4 minutes on medium speed. Pour batter into prepared pan.

3. Bake in preheated oven for 50 to 60 minutes. Let cool in pan for 10 minutes, then turn out onto a wire rack and cool completely.

4. In a saucepan over medium heat, cook 1/3 cup orange juice, sugar and butter for two minutes. Drizzle over cake.

APPLE ENCHILADA DESSERT

Servings: 6 | Prep: 15m | Cooks: 20m | Total: 35m

NUTRITION FACTS

Calories: 484 | Carbohydrates: 88.3g | Fat: 13.5g | Protein: 4.5g | Cholesterol: 0mg

INGREDIENTS

- 1 (21 ounce) can apple pie filling
- 1/2 cup white sugar
- 6 (8 inch) flour tortillas
- 1/2 cup packed brown sugar
- 1 teaspoon ground cinnamon
- 1/2 cup water
- 1/3 cup margarine

DIRECTIONS

1. Preheat oven to 350 degrees F (175 degrees C).
2. Spoon fruit evenly onto all tortillas, sprinkle with cinnamon. Roll up tortillas and place seam side down on lightly greased 8x8 baking pan.
3. Bring margarine, sugars and water to a boil in a medium sauce pan. Reduce heat and simmer, stirring constantly for 3 minutes.
4. Pour sauce evenly over tortillas; sprinkle with extra cinnamon on top if desired. Bake in preheated oven for 20 minutes.
5. Makes 6 large tortillas; may be cut in half to serve 12.

MARBLED PUMPKIN CHEESECAKE

Servings: 12 | Prep: 30m | Cooks: 1h10m | Total: 7h40m | Additional: 6h

NUTRITION FACTS

Calories: 350 | Carbohydrates: 26.8g | Fat: 25.3g | Protein: 5.8 g | Cholesterol: 101mg

INGREDIENTS

- 1 1/2 cups crushed gingersnap cookies
- 1 teaspoon vanilla extract
- 1/2 cup finely chopped pecans
- 3 eggs
- 1/3 cup butter, melted
- 1 cup canned pumpkin
- 2 (8 ounce) packages cream cheese, softened
- 3/4 teaspoon ground cinnamon
- 3/4 cup white sugar, divided
- 1/4 teaspoon ground nutmeg

DIRECTIONS

1. Preheat oven to 350 degrees F (175 degrees C). In a medium bowl, mix together the crushed gingersnap cookies, pecans, and butter. Press into the bottom, and about 1 inch up the sides of a 9 inch springform pan. Bake crust 10 minutes in the preheated oven. Set aside to cool.
2. In a medium bowl, mix together the cream cheese, 1/2 cup sugar, and vanilla just until smooth. Mix in eggs one at a time, blending well after each. Set aside 1 cup of the mixture. Blend 1/4 cup sugar, pumpkin, cinnamon, and nutmeg into the remaining mixture.
3. Spread the pumpkin flavored batter into the crust, and drop the plain batter by spoonfuls onto the top. Swirl with a knife to create a marbled effect.
4. Bake 55 minutes in the preheated oven, or until filling is set. Run a knife around the edge of the pan. Allow to cool before removing pan rim. Chill for at least 4 hours before serving.

BLACK BOTTOM CUPCAKES

Servings: 24 | Prep: 30m | Cooks: 30m | Total: 1h

NUTRITION FACTS

Calories: 171 | Carbohydrates: 22.4g | Fat: 8.9g | Protein: 2.3g | Cholesterol: 18mg

INGREDIENTS

- 1 (8 ounce) package cream cheese, softened
- 1/4 cup unsweetened cocoa powder
- 1 egg
- 1 teaspoon baking soda
- 1/3 cup white sugar
- 1/2 teaspoon salt
- 1/8 teaspoon salt
- 1 cup water
- 1 cup miniature semisweet chocolate chips
- 1/3 cup vegetable oil
- 1 1/2 cups all-purpose flour
- 1 tablespoon cider vinegar
- 1 cup white sugar
- 1 teaspoon vanilla extract

DIRECTIONS

1. Preheat oven to 350 degrees F (175 degrees C). Line muffin tins with paper cups or lightly spray with non-stick cooking spray.
2. In a medium bowl, beat the cream cheese, egg, 1/3 cup sugar and 1/8 teaspoon salt until light and fluffy. Stir in the chocolate chips and set aside.

3. In a large bowl, mix together the flour, 1 cup sugar, cocoa, baking soda and 1/2 teaspoon salt. Make a well in the center and add the water, oil, vinegar and vanilla. Stir together until well blended. Fill muffin tins 1/3 full with the batter and top with a dollop of the cream cheese mixture.

4. Bake in preheated oven for 25 to 30 minutes.

BLACK BOTTOM CUPCAKES

Servings: 15 | Prep: 15m | Cooks: 45m | Total: 1h

NUTRITION FACTS

Calories: 318 | Carbohydrates: 45.3g | Fat: 14.4g | Protein: 3.3g | Cholesterol: 12mg

INGREDIENTS

- 1 cup white sugar
- 1/4 teaspoon salt (optional)
- 1 teaspoon baking powder
- 1 pinch ground cinnamon (optional)
- 3 cups all-purpose flour
- 4 cups fresh blueberries
- 1 cup shortening
- 1/2 cup white sugar
- 1 egg
- 3 teaspoons cornstarch

DIRECTIONS

1. Preheat the oven to 375 degrees F (190 degrees C). Grease a 9x13 inch pan.

2. In a medium bowl, stir together 1 cup sugar, 3 cups flour, and baking powder. Mix in salt and cinnamon, if desired. Use a fork or pastry cutter to blend in the shortening and egg. Dough will be crumbly. Pat half of dough into the prepared pan.

3. In another bowl, stir together the sugar and cornstarch. Gently mix in the blueberries. Sprinkle the blueberry mixture evenly over the crust. Crumble remaining dough over the berry layer.

4. Bake in preheated oven for 45 minutes, or until top is slightly brown. Cool completely before cutting into squares.

SPOOKY WITCHES' FINGERS

Servings: 60 | Prep: 35m | Cooks: 20m | Total: 1h15m | Additional: 20m

NUTRITION FACTS

INGREDIENTS

- 1 cup butter, softened
- 2 2/3 cups all-purpose flour
- 1 cup confectioners' sugar
- 1 teaspoon baking powder
- 1 egg
- 1 teaspoon salt
- 1 teaspoon almond extract
- 3/4 cup whole almonds
- 1 teaspoon vanilla extract
- 1 (.75 ounce) tube red decorating gel

DIRECTIONS

1. Combine the butter, sugar, egg, almond extract, and vanilla extract in a mixing bowl. Beat together with an electric mixer; gradually add the flour, baking powder, and salt, continually beating; refrigerate 20 to 30 minutes.
2. Preheat oven to 325 degrees F (165 degrees C). Lightly grease baking sheets.
3. Remove dough from refrigerator in small amounts. Scoop 1 heaping teaspoon at a time onto a piece of waxed paper. Use the waxed paper to roll the dough into a thin finger-shaped cookie. Press one almond into one end of each cookie to give the appearance of a long fingernail. Squeeze cookie near the tip and again near the center of each to give the impression of knuckles. You can also cut into the dough with a sharp knife at the same points to help give a more finger-like appearance. Arrange the shaped cookies on the baking sheets.
4. Bake in the preheated oven until the cookies are slightly golden in color, 20 to 25 minutes.
5. Remove the almond from the end of each cookie; squeeze a small amount of red decorating gel into the cavity; replace the almond to cause the gel to ooze out around the tip of the cookie.

FRESH STRAWBERRY UPSIDE DOWN CAKE
Servings: 12 | Prep: 15m | Cooks: 50m | Total: 1h20m | Additional: 15m

NUTRITION FACTS

Calories: 290 | Carbohydrates: 58.3g | Fat: 5g | Protein: 3.1g | Cholesterol: 1mg

INGREDIENTS

- 2 cups crushed fresh strawberries
- 3 cups miniature marshmallows

* 1 (6 ounce) package strawberry flavored Jell-O mix
* 1 (18 ounce) package yellow cake mix, batter prepared as directed on package

DIRECTIONS

1. Preheat an oven to 350 degrees F (175 degrees C).
2. Spread crushed strawberries on the bottom of a 9x13 inch baking pan. Evenly sprinkle strawberries with the dry gelatin powder, and top with mini marshmallows.
3. Prepare the cake mix as directed on the package, and pour on top of the marshmallows. Bake in the preheated oven until a toothpick inserted into the center comes out clean, about 40 to 50 minutes. Cool in the pan for 15 minutes. Run a knife around the pan to loosen the sides, and turn the cake out onto a serving tray. Store cake in the refrigerator.

HOT FUDGE ICE CREAM BAR DESSERT
Servings: 12 | Prep: 30m | Cooks: 2m | Total: 1h35m

NUTRITION FACTS

Calories: 575 | Carbohydrates: 70.7g | Fat: 28.1g | Protein: 11.9g | Cholesterol: 31mg

INGREDIENTS

* 1 (16 ounce) can chocolate syrup
* 1 (12 ounce) container frozen whipped topping, thawed
* 3/4 cup peanut butter
* 1 cup salted peanuts
* 19 ice cream sandwiches

DIRECTIONS

1. Pour the chocolate syrup into a medium microwave-safe bowl and microwave until hot, about 2 minutes on high, stopping every 30 seconds. Do not allow to boil. Stir peanut butter into hot chocolate until smooth. Allow to cool to room temperature.
2. Line the bottom of a 9x13-inch dish with a layer of ice cream sandwiches. Spread half the whipped topping over the sandwiches. Spoon half the chocolate mixture over that. Top with half the peanuts. Repeat layers. Freeze until firm, at least 1 hour. Cut into squares to serve.

URBAN LEGEND CHOCOLATE CHIP COOKIES
Servings: 60 | Prep: 15m | Cooks: 8m | Total: 23m

NUTRITION FACTS

Calories: 141 | Carbohydrates: 17.5g | Fat: 7.7g | Protein: 2g | Cholesterol: 15mg

INGREDIENTS

- 1 cup butter, softened
- 1/2 teaspoon salt
- 1 cup white sugar
- 1 teaspoon baking powder
- 1 cup packed brown sugar
- 1 teaspoon baking soda
- 2 eggs
- 2 cups semisweet chocolate chips
- 1 teaspoon vanilla extract
- 4 ounces milk chocolate, grated
- 2 cups all-purpose flour
- 1 1/2 cups chopped walnuts
- 2 1/2 cups rolled oats

DIRECTIONS

1. Preheat oven to 375 degrees F (190 degrees C). Measure oats into a blender or food processor, and then blend to a fine powder. Set aside.
2. In a large bowl, cream together butter and sugars. Beat in the eggs one at a time, then stir in the vanilla. In a separate bowl, mix together flour, oats, salt, baking powder, and baking soda. Stir dry ingredients into creamed butter and sugar. Add chocolate chips, grated chocolate, and nuts.
3. Drop by rounded teaspoons onto ungreased cookie sheets. Bake for 6 to 8 minutes in the preheated oven.

CLASSIC TIRAMISU

Servings: 12 | Prep: 30m | Cooks: 30m | Total: 2h

NUTRITION FACTS

Calories: 568 | Carbohydrates: 59.6g | Fat: 31.8g | Protein: 9.8g | Cholesterol: 303mg

INGREDIENTS

- 6 egg yolks
- 2 (12 ounce) packages ladyfingers
- 1 1/4 cups white sugar
- 1/3 cup coffee flavored liqueur
- 1 1/4 cups mascarpone cheese
- 1 teaspoon unsweetened cocoa powder, for dusting
- 1 3/4 cups heavy whipping cream

- 1 (1 ounce) square semisweet chocolate

DIRECTIONS

1. Combine egg yolks and sugar in the top of a double boiler, over boiling water. Reduce heat to low, and cook for about 10 minutes, stirring constantly. Remove from heat and whip yolks until thick and lemon colored.
2. Add mascarpone to whipped yolks. Beat until combined. In a separate bowl, whip cream to stiff peaks. Gently fold into yolk mixture and set aside.
3. Split the lady fingers in half, and line the bottom and sides of a large glass bowl. Brush with coffee liqueur. Spoon half of the cream filling over the lady fingers. Repeat ladyfingers, coffee liqueur and filling layers. Garnish with cocoa and chocolate curls. Refrigerate several hours or overnight.
4. To make the chocolate curls, use a vegetable peeler and run it down the edge of the chocolate bar.

PUMPKIN PIE

Servings: 8 | Prep: 15m | Cooks: 45m | Total: 1h

NUTRITION FACTS

Calories: 320 | Carbohydrates: 41.9g | Fat: 14.2g | Protein: 7.6g | Cholesterol: 117mg

INGREDIENTS

- 1 (15 ounce) can pumpkin puree
- 1/2 teaspoon ground ginger
- 3 egg yolks
- 1/2 teaspoon fine salt
- 1 large egg
- 1/4 teaspoon freshly grated nutmeg
- 1 (14 ounce) can sweetened condensed milk
- 1/8 teaspoon Chinese 5-spice powder
- 1 teaspoon ground cinnamon
- 1 9-inch unbaked pie crust (see footnote for recipe link)

DIRECTIONS

1. Preheat oven to 425 degrees F (220 degrees C).
2. Whisk together pumpkin puree, egg yolks, and egg in a large bowl until smooth. Add sweetened condensed milk, cinnamon, ginger, salt, nutmeg, and Chinese 5-spice powder; whisk until thoroughly combined.
3. Fit pie crust in a 9-inch pie plate and crimp edges.
4. Pour filling into the pie shell and lightly tap on the work surface to release any air bubbles.
5. Bake in the preheated oven for 15 minutes.

6. Reduce heat to 350 degrees F (175 degrees C) and bake until just set in the middle, 30 to 40 more minutes. A paring knife inserted into the filling, 1 inch from the crust, should come out clean. Allow to cool completely before serving.

CREAMY BLUEBERRY PIE

Servings: 8 | Prep: 25m | Cooks: 55m | Total: 2h20m | Additional: 1h

NUTRITION FACTS

Calories: 440 | Carbohydrates: 67.3g | Fat: 17.8g | Protein: 4.8g | Cholesterol: 68mg

INGREDIENTS

- 3 cups fresh blueberries
- 2 eggs, beaten
- 1 (9 inch) deep dish pie crust
- 1/2 cup sour cream
- 1 cup white sugar
- 1/2 cup white sugar
- 1/3 cup all-purpose flour
- 1/2 cup all-purpose flour
- 1/8 teaspoon salt
- 1/4 cup butter

DIRECTIONS

1. Preheat oven to 350 degrees F (175 degrees C). Place the blueberries in the pastry shell and set aside.
2. Combine 1 cup sugar, 1/3 cup flour, and salt. Add eggs and sour cream, stirring until blended. Pour the sour cream custard over the blueberries.
3. In another bowl, combine 1/2 cup sugar and 1/2 cup flour. Cut in the butter with pastry blender until the mixture resembles coarse meal. Sprinkle the topping over the sour cream mixture and berries in the pie shell.
4. Bake in the preheated oven for 50 to 55 minutes, or until lightly browned. Cool on wire rack.

STREUSEL TOPPED BLUEBERRY MUFFINS

Servings: 12 | Prep: 20m | Cooks: 25m | Total: 45m

NUTRITION FACTS

Calories: 266 | Carbohydrates: 38.9g | Fat: 10.9g | Protein: 4g | Cholesterol: 0mg

INGREDIENTS

- 2 cups all-purpose flour
- 1 teaspoon vanilla extract
- 2 teaspoons baking powder
- 1/4 teaspoon lemon zest
- 1/2 teaspoon salt
- 1/2 cup milk
- 1 1/2 tablespoons all-purpose flour
- 2 tablespoons all-purpose flour
- 1 1/2 cups fresh blueberries
- 5 tablespoons white sugar
- 1/2 cup butter
- 1/2 teaspoon ground cinnamon
- 3/4 cup white sugar
- 2 tablespoons butter, diced
- 2 eggs

DIRECTIONS

1. Preheat oven to 375 degrees F (190 degrees C). Grease 12 muffin cups or line with paper muffin liners.

2. Combine 2 cups flour, 2 teaspoons baking powder, and 1/2 teaspoon salt in medium bowl. In a small bowl, sprinkle 1 to 2 tablespoons flour over blueberries, and set aside. (This simple trick will keep you from having "purple" batter).

3. In a large bowl, beat 1/2 cup butter with 3/4 cup sugar until light and fluffy. Beat in eggs, and stir in vanilla and lemon zest. Fold in dry ingredients alternately with milk. Fold in blueberries. Remember, fold gently, don't stir. Spoon batter into prepared cups.

4. Combine 2 tablespoons flour, 5 tablespoons sugar ,and 1/2 teaspoon cinnamon in a small bowl. Cut in 2 tablespoons butter with fork or pastry blender until mixture resembles course crumbs. Sprinkle over batter in muffin cups.

5. Bake in the preheated oven for 20 to 25 minutes, or until a toothpick inserted in center of a muffin comes out clean. Cool in pans on wire rack. These muffins freeze really well, and re-heat in the microwave successfully. Hope you enjoy!!

APPLE TURNOVERS

Servings: 8 | Prep: 30m | Cooks: 25m | Total: 55m

NUTRITION FACTS

Calories: 562 | Carbohydrates: 80g | Fat: 25.9g | Protein: 4.8g | Cholesterol: 8mg

INGREDIENTS

- 2 tablespoons lemon juice
- 1 tablespoon cornstarch
- 4 cups water
- 1 tablespoon water
- 4 Granny Smith apples - peeled, cored and sliced
- 1 (17.25 ounce) package frozen puff pastry sheets, thawed
- 2 tablespoons butter
- 1 cup confectioners' sugar
- 1 cup brown sugar
- 1 tablespoon milk
- 1 teaspoon ground cinnamon
- 1 teaspoon vanilla extract

DIRECTIONS

1. Combine the lemon and 4 cups water in a large bowl. Place the sliced apples in the water to keep them from browning.
2. Melt butter in a large skillet over medium heat. Drain water from apples, and place them into the hot skillet. Cook and stir for about 2 minutes. Add brown sugar, and cinnamon, and cook, stirring, for 2 more minutes. Stir together cornstarch and 1 tablespoon water. Pour into the skillet, and mix well. Cook for another minute, or until sauce has thickened. Remove from heat to cool slightly.
3. Preheat the oven to 400 degrees F (200 degrees C).
4. Unfold puff pastry sheets, and repair any cracks by pressing them back together. Trim each sheet into a square. Then cut each larger square into 4 smaller squares. Spoon apples onto the center of each squares. Fold over from corner to corner into a triangle shape, and press edges together to seal. Place turnovers on a baking sheet, leaving about 1 inch between them.
5. Bake for 25 minutes in the preheated oven, until turnovers are puffed and lightly browned. Cool completely before glazing.
6. To make the glaze, mix together the confectioners' sugar, milk and vanilla in a small bowl. Adjust the thickness by adding more sugar or milk if necessary. Drizzle glaze over the cooled turnovers.

AMAZING PECAN COFFEE CAKE

Servings: 12 | Prep: 20m | Cooks: 30m | Total: 50m

NUTRITION FACTS

Calories: 485 | Carbohydrates: 52.7g | Fat: 29.5g | Protein: 4.9g | Cholesterol: 85mg

INGREDIENTS

- 2 cups all-purpose flour
- 2 eggs
- 1/4 teaspoon salt
- 1 tablespoon vanilla extract
- 1 tablespoon baking powder

- 1/2 cup brown sugar
- 1 cup butter, softened
- 1 cup chopped pecans
- 1 cup sour cream
- 1 teaspoon ground cinnamon
- 1 1/2 cups white sugar
- 2 tablespoons butter, melted

DIRECTIONS

1. Preheat oven to 350 degrees F (175 degrees C). Line a 9x13 inch pan with aluminum foil, and lightly grease with vegetable oil or cooking spray. Sift together the flour, baking powder, and salt; set aside.
2. In a large bowl, cream the butter until light and fluffy. Gradually beat in sour cream, then beat in sugar. Beat in the eggs one at a time, then stir in the vanilla. By hand, fold in the flour mixture, mixing just until incorporated. Spread batter into prepared pan.
3. To make the Pecan Topping: In a medium bowl, mix together brown sugar, pecans and cinnamon. Stir in melted butter until crumbly. Sprinkle over cake batter in pan.
4. Bake in the preheated oven for 30 to 35 minutes, or until a toothpick inserted into the center of the cake comes out clean. Let cool in pan for 10 minutes, then turn out onto a wire rack, and remove foil.

SOUR CREAM COFFEE CAKE

Servings: 18 | Prep: 15m | Cooks: 40m | Total: 55m

NUTRITION FACTS

Calories: 306 | Carbohydrates: 41.4g | Fat: 14.9g | Protein: 2.9g | Cholesterol: 57mg

INGREDIENTS

- 1 cup butter
- 1 teaspoon baking powder
- 2 cups white sugar
- 1/8 teaspoon salt
- 2 eggs
- 1/3 cup all-purpose flour
- 1 cup sour cream
- 1/2 cup packed brown sugar
- 1/2 teaspoon vanilla extract
- 2 tablespoons melted butter
- 2 cups all-purpose flour

- 1 teaspoon ground cinnamon

DIRECTIONS

1. Preheat oven to 350 degrees F (175 degrees C). Grease a 9x13 inch baking pan.
2. In a large bowl, cream together 1 cup butter and white sugar until light and fluffy. Beat in the eggs one at a time, then stir in the sour cream and vanilla. Mix in 2 cups flour, baking powder, and salt. Spread 1/2 of batter in the prepared pan.
3. Prepare the filling: In a medium bowl mix 1/3 cup flour, brown sugar, 2 tablespoons melted butter, and cinnamon. Sprinkle cake batter with 1/2 the filling. Spread second half of batter over the filling, and top with remaining filling.
4. Bake 35 to 40 minutes in the preheated oven, or until a toothpick inserted near the center comes out clean.

CARAMEL PECAN PIE

Servings: 8 | Prep: 30m | Cooks: 50m | Total: 1h20m

NUTRITION FACTS

Calories: 535 | Carbohydrates: 66.4g | Fat: 28.6g | Protein: 7.4g | Cholesterol: 89mg

INGREDIENTS

- 1 (9 inch) unbaked pie crust
- 3 eggs
- 36 individually wrapped caramels, unwrapped
- 1/2 teaspoon vanilla extract
- 1/4 cup butter
- 1/4 teaspoon salt
- 1/4 cup milk
- 1 cup pecan halves
- 3/4 cup white sugar

DIRECTIONS

1. Preheat oven to 350 degrees F (175 degrees C.) In a saucepan over low heat, combine caramels, butter and milk. Cook, stirring frequently, until smooth. Remove from heat and set aside.
2. In a large bowl, combine sugar, eggs, vanilla and salt. Gradually mix in the melted caramel mixture. Stir in pecans. Pour filling into unbaked pie crust.
3. Bake in the preheated oven for 45 to 50 minutes, or until pastry is golden brown. Allow to cool until filling is firm.

CARROT CAKE

Servings: 15 | Prep: 30m | Cooks: 55m | Total: 2h | Additional: 35m

NUTRITION FACTS

Calories: 616 | Carbohydrates: 83.5g | Fat: 30.2g | Protein: 6.2g | Cholesterol: 70mg

INGREDIENTS

- 2 cups white sugar
- 2 teaspoons baking soda
- 3/4 cup vegetable oil
- 2 teaspoons ground cinnamon
- 3 eggs
- 1 1/2 teaspoons salt
- 1 teaspoon vanilla extract
- 1 cup chopped walnuts
- 3/4 cup buttermilk
- 1/2 cup butter
- 2 cups grated carrots
- 1 (8 ounce) package cream cheese
- 1 cup flaked coconut
- 1 teaspoon vanilla extract
- 1 (15 ounce) can crushed pineapple, drained
- 4 cups confectioners' sugar
- 2 cups all-purpose flour

DIRECTIONS

1. Preheat oven to 350 degrees F (175 degrees C). Grease a 9x13 inch baking pan. Set aside.
2. In a large bowl, mix together sugar, oil, eggs, vanilla, and buttermilk. Stir in carrots, coconut, vanilla, and pineapple. In a separate bowl, combine flour, baking soda, cinnamon, and salt; gently stir into carrot mixture. Stir in chopped nuts. Spread batter into prepared pan.
3. Bake for 55 minutes or until toothpick inserted into cake comes out clean. Remove from oven, and set aside to cool.
4. In a medium mixing bowl, combine butter or margarine, cream cheese, vanilla, and confectioners sugar. Blend until creamy. Frost cake while still in the pan.

TEXAS SHEET CAKE

Servings: 32 | Prep: 10m | Cooks: 20m | Total: 30m

NUTRITION FACTS

Calories: 256 | Carbohydrates: 35.8g | Fat: 12.5g | Protein: 2.4g | Cholesterol: 36mg

INGREDIENTS

- 2 cups all-purpose flour
- 5 tablespoons unsweetened cocoa powder
- 2 cups white sugar
- 6 tablespoons milk
- 1 teaspoon baking soda
- 5 tablespoons unsweetened cocoa powder
- 1/2 teaspoon salt
- 1/2 cup butter
- 1/2 cup sour cream
- 4 cups confectioners' sugar
- 2 eggs
- 1 teaspoon vanilla extract
- 1 cup butter
- 1 cup chopped walnuts (optional)
- 1 cup water

DIRECTIONS

1. Preheat oven to 350 degrees F (175 degrees C). Grease and flour a 10x15 inch pan.
2. Combine the flour, sugar, baking soda and salt. Beat in the sour cream and eggs. Set aside. Melt the butter on low in a saucepan, add the water and 5 tablespoons cocoa. Bring mixture to a boil then remove from heat. Allow to cool slightly, then stir cocoa mixture into the egg mixture, mixing until blended.
3. Pour batter into prepared pan. Bake in the preheated oven for 20 minutes, or until a toothpick inserted into the center comes out clean.
4. For the icing: In a large saucepan, combine the milk, 5 tablespoons cocoa and 1/2 cup butter. Bring to a boil, then remove from heat. Stir in the confectioners' sugar and vanilla, then fold in the nuts, mixing until blended. Spread frosting over warm cake.

CHEESECAKE SUPREME

Servings: 12 | Prep: 30m | Cooks: 1h10m | Total: 1h40m

NUTRITION FACTS

Calories: 610 | Carbohydrates: 49.4g | Fat: 42.1g | Protein: 11.1g | Cholesterol: 231mg

INGREDIENTS

- 1 1/2 cups graham cracker crumbs
- 2 egg yolks
- 1/2 cup white sugar
- 1 3/4 cups white sugar
- 1/4 cup butter, melted
- 1/8 cup all-purpose flour
- 5 (8 ounce) packages cream cheese, softened
- 1/4 cup heavy whipping cream
- 5 eggs

DIRECTIONS

1. Preheat oven to 400 degrees F (200 degrees C).
2. Mix the graham cracker crumbs, 1/2 cup of the white sugar, and the melted butter together. Press mixture into the bottom of one 9 or 10 inch springform pan.
3. In a large bowl, combine cream cheese, eggs and egg yolks; mix until smooth. Add the remaining 1 3/4 cups white sugar, the flour and the heavy cream. Blend until smooth. Pour batter into prepared pan.
4. Bake at 400 degrees F (200 degrees C) for 10 minutes, then turn oven temperature down to 200 degrees F (100 degrees C) and continue baking for 1 hour, or until filling is set. Let cheesecake cool, then refrigerate.

CAKE MIXES FROM SCRATCH AND VARIATIONS
Servings: 24 | Prep: 20m | Cooks: 35m | Total: 55m

NUTRITION FACTS

Calories: 142 | Carbohydrates: 22.5g | Fat: 5g | Protein: 2.1g | Cholesterol: 16mg

INGREDIENTS

- 2 1/3 cups all-purpose flour
- 1/2 cup shortening
- 1 tablespoon baking powder
- 2 eggs
- 3/4 teaspoon salt
- 1 cup milk
- 1 1/2 cups white sugar
- 1 teaspoon vanilla extract

DIRECTIONS

1. For a Yellow Cake: Sift together flour, baking powder, salt, and sugar. Cut in shortening until fine crumbs are formed. Add eggs, milk, and vanilla. Beat at low speed for 1 minute, then high for 2 minutes, scraping the bowl frequently.

2. Pour batter into greased and floured 9x13 inch pan. Bake in preheated 350 degree F oven (175 degrees C) for 25 to 30 minutes.

3. Variation for a White Cake: Prepare as for the basic cake except use 3 egg whites for the 2 whole eggs. Whites may be beaten separately and added for a lighter cake.

4. Variation for a Chocolate Cake: Add 1/4 cup cocoa powder to the basic cake mix prior to adding the milk.

5. Variation for a Spice Cake: Add 1 teaspoon cinnamon, 1/4 teaspoon ground cloves, and 1/4 teaspoon ground allspice to the basic cake mix.

6. Variation for a Pineapple Upside Down Cake: Melt 1/2 cup butter in the bottom of a 9x13 pan. Add 2/3 cup brown sugar, stirring into the butter. Arrange pineapple slices in the pan. Top with the basic (yellow cake) mix recipe. Bake 30 to 35 minutes, cool 5 minutes, and invert to serve.

CHOCOLATE CHOCOLATE CHIP COOKIES

Servings: 12 | Prep: 20m | Cooks: 10m | Total: 1h | Additional: 30m

NUTRITION FACTS

Calories: 467 | Carbohydrates: 61.6g | Fat: 25.2g | Protein: 5.2g | Cholesterol: 72mg

INGREDIENTS

- 2 cups all-purpose flour
- 3/4 cup packed brown sugar
- 1/2 cup cocoa powder
- 2 eggs
- 1 teaspoon baking soda
- 1 teaspoon vanilla extract
- 1 cup softened butter
- 2 cups semisweet chocolate chips
- 3/4 cup white sugar

DIRECTIONS

1. Preheat oven to 350 degrees F (175 degrees C). Whisk together the flour, cocoa powder, and baking soda.

2. Beat the butter, white sugar, and brown sugar with an electric mixer in a large bowl until smooth. Beat in one egg until completely incorporated. Beat in the last egg along with the vanilla. Mix in the

flour mixture until just incorporated. Fold in the chocolate chips; mixing just enough to evenly combine. Drop by heaped teaspoonfuls onto ungreased baking sheets.

3. Bake in the preheated oven until the edges are golden, 9 to 12 minutes. Allow the cookies to cool on the baking sheet for 1 minute before removing to a wire rack to cool completely.

PECAN PIE
Servings: 8 | Prep: 10m | Cooks: 1h | Total: 1h10m

NUTRITION FACTS

Calories: 512 | Carbohydrates: 65.1g | Fat: 27.3g | Protein: 5.4g | Cholesterol: 85mg

INGREDIENTS

- 1 3/4 cups white sugar
- 3 eggs
- 1/4 cup dark corn syrup
- 1/4 teaspoon salt
- 1/4 cup butter
- 1 teaspoon vanilla extract
- 1 tablespoon cold water
- 1 ¼ cups chopped pecans
- 2 teaspoons cornstarch
- 1 (9 inch) unbaked pie shell

DIRECTIONS

1. Preheat oven to 350 degrees F (175 degrees C).
2. In a medium saucepan, combine the sugar, corn syrup, butter, water, and cornstarch. Bring to a full boil, and remove from heat.
3. In a large bowl, beat eggs until frothy. Gradually beat in cooked syrup mixture. Stir in salt, vanilla, and pecans. Pour into pie shell.
4. Bake in preheated oven for 45 to 50 minutes, or until filling is set.

FLOURLESS CHOCOLATE CAKE
Servings: 8 | Prep: 15m | Cooks: 30m | Total: 1h55m | Additional: 1h10

NUTRITION FACTS

Calories: 285 | Carbohydrates: 29.9g | Fat: 18.6g | Protein: 4.5g | Cholesterol: 100mg

INGREDIENTS

- 4 (1 ounce) squares semisweet chocolate, chopped
- 1/2 cup cocoa powder
- 1/2 cup butter
- 3 eggs, beaten
- 3/4 cup white sugar
- 1 teaspoon vanilla extract

DIRECTIONS

1. Preheat oven to 300 degrees F (150 degrees C). Grease an 8 inch round cake pan, and dust with cocoa powder.
2. In the top of a double boiler over lightly simmering water, melt chocolate and butter. Remove from heat, and stir in sugar, cocoa powder, eggs, and vanilla. Pour into prepared pan.
3. Bake in preheated oven for 30 minutes. Let cool in pan for 10 minutes, then turn out onto a wire rack and cool completely. Slices can also be reheated for 20 to 30 seconds in the microwave before serving.

CINNAMON-ROASTED ALMONDS

Servings: 16 | Prep: 15m | Cooks: 1h | Total: 1h15m

NUTRITION FACTS

Calories: 231 | Carbohydrates: 13.3g | Fat: 18g | Protein: 7.8g | Cholesterol: 0mg

INGREDIENTS

- 1 egg white
- 1/2 cup white sugar
- 1 teaspoon cold water
- 1/4 teaspoon salt
- 4 cups whole almonds
- 1/2 teaspoon ground cinnamon

DIRECTIONS

1. Preheat oven to 250 degrees F (120 degrees C). Lightly grease a 10x15 inch jellyroll pan.
2. Lightly beat the egg white; add water, and beat until frothy but not stiff. Add the nuts, and stir until well coated. Mix the sugar, salt, and cinnamon, and sprinkle over the nuts. Toss to coat, and spread evenly on the prepared pan.
3. Bake for 1 hour in the preheated oven, stirring occasionally, until golden. Allow to cool, then store nuts in airtight containers.

HOMEMADE FRESH PUMPKIN PIE

Servings: 8 | Prep: 20m | Cooks: 40m | Total: 1h

NUTRITION FACTS

Calories: 363 | Carbohydrates: 44.3g | Fat: 18g | Protein: 7.4g | Cholesterol: 60mg

INGREDIENTS

- 1 1/3 cups all-purpose flour
- 2 eggs, beaten
- 1/2 teaspoon salt
- 3/4 cup packed brown sugar
- 1/2 cup shortening
- 1/2 teaspoon ground cinnamon
- 3 1/2 tablespoons cold water
- 1/2 teaspoon ground ginger
- 2 cups mashed, cooked pumpkin
- 1/2 teaspoon ground nutmeg
- 1 (12 fluid ounce) can evaporated milk
- 1/2 teaspoon salt

DIRECTIONS

1. Preheat oven to 400 degrees F (200 degrees C).
2. Prepare pie crust by mixing together the flour and salt. Cut shortening into flour; add cold water 1 tablespoon at a time (you may need only 3 tablespoons, or up to 4 tablespoons). Mix dough and repeat until dough is moist enough to hold together.
3. With lightly floured, hands shape dough into a ball. On a lightly floured board roll dough out to about 1/8 inch thickness. With a sharp knife, cut dough 1 1/2 inch larger than the upside-down 8- to 9-inch pie pan. Gently roll the dough around the rolling pin and transfer it right-side up onto the pie pan. Unroll, easing dough into the bottom of the pie pan.
4. In a large bowl, beat pumpkin with evaporated milk, eggs, brown sugar, cinnamon, ginger, nutmeg and salt with an electric mixer or immersion blender. Mix well. Pour into a prepared crust. Bake 40 minutes or until when a knife is inserted 1 inch from the edge comes out clean.

BUTTERMILK POUND CAKE

Servings: 12 | Prep: 15m | Cooks: 1h30m | Total: 1h45m

NUTRITION FACTS

Calories: 489 | Carbohydrates: 75.1g | Fat: 18.3g | Protein: 7.2g | Cholesterol: 134mg

INGREDIENTS

- 3 cups all-purpose flour
- 6 eggs
- 1/4 teaspoon baking soda
- 1 teaspoon lemon extract
- 1/2 teaspoon salt
- 1 teaspoon vanilla extract
- 1 cup butter
- 1 cup buttermilk
- 3 cups white sugar

DIRECTIONS

1. Preheat oven to 325 degrees F (165 degrees C). Grease one 9 or 10 inch tube pan. Mix together the flour, baking soda, and salt. Set aside.
2. In a large bowl, beat butter with sugar. Mix in the eggs, one at time, beating well after each addition. Stir in the lemon and the vanilla extracts. Gently mix in flour mixture alternately with the buttermilk. Pour batter into the prepared pan.
3. Bake in preheated oven for 90 minutes. Do not open oven door until after one hour. When cake begins to pull away from the side of the pan it is done. Let cool in pan for 10 minutes, then turn out onto a wire rack and cool completely.

CREAMIEST RICE PUDDING

Servings: 12 | Prep: 10m | Cooks: 1h15m | Total: 8h

NUTRITION FACTS

Calories: 228 | Carbohydrates: 37.7g | Fat: 4.7g | Protein: 8.3g | Cholesterol: 60mg

INGREDIENTS

- 1/2 gallon milk
- 1/4 cup milk
- 1 cup white sugar
- 1/4 teaspoon salt
- 1 cup uncooked long-grain white rice
- 2 teaspoons vanilla extract
- 3 eggs, lightly beaten
- ground cinnamon to taste

DIRECTIONS

1. In a large saucepan over medium-low heat, combine 1/2 gallon milk, sugar and rice. Simmer, covered, 1 hour, stirring frequently. Remove pan from heat and let rest 10 minutes.
2. In a small bowl, combine eggs, 1/4 cup milk, salt and vanilla. Stir into rice mixture and return pot to low heat, stirring constantly, for 2 minutes. Pour into a 9x13 inch dish and cover with plastic wrap, folding back the corners to allow the steam to escape.
3. When pudding has cooled to room temperature, remove plastic wrap and sprinkle surface of pudding with cinnamon. Cover tightly (with fresh wrap) and refrigerate 8 hours or overnight before serving.

WHITE CHOCOLATE MACADAMIA NUT COOKIES

Servings: 24 | Prep: 15m | Cooks: 8m | Total: 23m

NUTRITION FACTS

Calories: 193 | Carbohydrates: 17.6g | Fat: 13.2g | Protein: 2.2g | Cholesterol: 20mg

INGREDIENTS

- 1/2 cup butter
- 1/2 teaspoon baking soda
- 3/4 cup white sugar
- 1/2 teaspoon salt
- 1 egg
- 8 ounces white chocolate, chopped
- 1 teaspoon vanilla extract
- 1 (6.5 ounce) jar macadamia nuts, chopped
- 1 ¼ cups all-purpose flour

DIRECTIONS

1. Preheat oven to 375 degrees F (190 degrees C).
2. In a medium bowl, cream together the butter and sugar. Stir in the egg and vanilla. Combine the flour, baking soda and salt, stir into the creamed mixture. Finally, stir in the white chocolate and nuts. Drop cookies by heaping teaspoonfuls onto an ungreased cookie sheet, about 2 inches apart.
3. Bake for 8 to 10 minutes in the preheated oven, until lightly browned. Cool on wire racks. When cool, store in an airtight container.

WHITE CHOCOLATE, CHOCOLATE COOKIES

Servings: 36 | Prep: 25m | Cooks: 10m | Total: 35m

NUTRITION FACTS

Calories: 173 | Carbohydrates: 22g | Fat: 9.4g | Protein: 2.3g | Cholesterol: 26mg

INGREDIENTS

- 1 cup unsalted butter
- 1 1/4 cups unsweetened cocoa powder
- 1 cup white sugar
- 1 3/4 cups all-purpose flour
- 3/4 cup packed brown sugar
- 2 teaspoons baking soda
- 2 eggs
- 2 cups white chocolate chips

DIRECTIONS

1. Preheat oven to 350 degrees F (175 degrees C). Grease cookie sheets.
2. In a large bowl, cream together the butter, brown sugar and white sugar until light and fluffy. Add the eggs one at a time, beating well with each addition. Combine the cocoa, flour, and baking soda, gradually stir into the creamed mixture. Finally, fold in white chocolate chips. Drop by rounded spoonfuls onto the prepared cookie sheets.
3. Bake for 8 to 10 minutes in the preheated oven, until puffy but still soft. Allow cookies to cool on baking sheet for 5 minutes before removing to a wire rack to cool completely.

PEANUT BLOSSOMS

Servings: 84 | Prep: 30m | Cooks: 12m | Total: 1h30m | Additional: 48m

NUTRITION FACTS

Calories: 116 | Carbohydrates: 14.3g | Fat: 6g | Protein: 1.9g | Cholesterol: 6mg

INGREDIENTS

- 1 cup shortening
- 2 teaspoons vanilla extract
- 1 cup peanut butter
- 3 1/2 cups all-purpose flour
- 1 cup packed brown sugar
- 2 teaspoons baking soda
- 1 cup white sugar
- 1 teaspoon salt
- 2 eggs
- 1/2 cup white sugar for decoration
- 1/4 cup milk
- 2 (9 ounce) bags milk chocolate candy kisses, unwrapped

DIRECTIONS

1. Preheat oven to 375 degrees F (190 degrees C). Grease cookie sheets.
2. In a large bowl, cream together the shortening, peanut butter, brown sugar, and 1 cup white sugar until smooth. Beat in the eggs one at a time, and stir in the milk and vanilla. Combine the flour, baking soda, and salt; stir into the peanut butter mixture until well blended. Shape tablespoonfuls of dough into balls, and roll in remaining white sugar. Place cookies 2 inches apart on the prepared cookie sheets.
3. Bake for 10 to12 minutes in the preheated oven. Remove from oven, and immediately press a chocolate kiss into each cookie. Allow to cool completely; the kiss will harden as it cools.

PEACH PIE
Servings: 8 | Prep: 1h | Cooks: 45m | Total: 1h45m

NUTRITION FACTS

Calories: 425 | Carbohydrates: 57g | Fat: 20.7g | Protein: 3.4g | Cholesterol: 15mg

INGREDIENTS

- 10 fresh peaches, pitted and sliced
- 1/4 cup butter
- 1/3 cup all-purpose flour
- 1 recipe pastry for a 9 inch double crust pie
- 1 cup white sugar

DIRECTIONS

1. Mix flour, sugar and butter into crumb stage.
2. Place one crust in the bottom of a 9 inch pie plate. Line the shell with some sliced peaches. Sprinkle some of the butter mixture on top of the peaches, then put more peaches on top of the the crumb mixture. Continue layering until both the peaches and crumbs are gone.
3. Top with lattice strips of pie crust.
4. Bake at 350 degrees F (175 degrees C) for 45 minutes, or until crust is golden. Allow pie to cool before slicing. Best when eaten fresh.

CHUNKY CHEESECAKE BROWNIES
Servings: 16 | Prep: 25m | Cooks: 30m | Total: 55m

NUTRITION FACTS

Calories: 244 | Carbohydrates: 27.1g | Fat: 15g | Protein: 3.7g | Cholesterol: 58mg

INGREDIENTS

- 1 (8 ounce) package cream cheese, softened
- 1/2 cup white sugar
- 1/4 cup white sugar
- 2 eggs
- 1 egg
- 2/3 cup all-purpose flour
- 1 cup semisweet chocolate chips
- 1/2 teaspoon baking powder
- 1/4 cup butter
- 1/4 teaspoon salt
- 1 cup semisweet chocolate chips

DIRECTIONS

1. Preheat oven to 350 degrees F (175 degrees C). Grease a 9-inch square baking pan.
2. Combine cream cheese with 1/4 cup sugar and 1 egg in a mixing bowl; beat until smooth. Stir 1 cup chocolate chips into the cream cheese mixture. Set aside.
3. Fill a saucepan with water and bring to a boil. Turn the heat off, and set a heatproof mixing bowl over the water. In the mixing bowl, combine butter with the remaining cup of chocolate chips; stir until just melted and blended together. Stir in the remaining 1/2 cup sugar and 2 eggs, then sift together flour, baking powder, and salt; stir into chocolate until evenly blended.
4. Pour half of the batter into the prepared baking pan. Spread the cream cheese mixture over the chocolate layer. Top with remaining chocolate mixture (this doesn't need to completely cover the cream cheese layer). Using a knife, swirl the top chocolate layer into the cream cheese to make a marble pattern.
5. Bake in preheated oven at 350 degrees F (175 degrees C) for 25 to 30 minutes, or until top is crinkled and edges pull away from sides of the pan. Cool thoroughly. Cut into 12 to 16 squares. Store in the refrigerator or freeze.

PEACH PIE THE OLD FASHIONED TWO CRUST WAY
Servings: 8 | Prep: 30m | Cooks: 45m | Total: 1h15m

NUTRITION FACTS

Calories: 428 | Carbohydrates: 58.6g | Fat: 19.8g | Protein: 4.7g | Cholesterol: 31mg

INGREDIENTS

- 1 (15 ounce) package pastry for a 9 inch double crust pie
- 1 cup white sugar
- 1 egg, beaten
- 1/2 teaspoon ground cinnamon
- 5 cups sliced peeled peaches
- 1/4 teaspoon ground nutmeg
- 2 tablespoons lemon juice
- 1/4 teaspoon salt
- 1/2 cup all-purpose flour
- 2 tablespoons butter

DIRECTIONS

1. Preheat the oven to 450 degrees F (220 degrees C).
2. Line the bottom and sides of a 9 inch pie plate with one of the pie crusts. Brush with some of the beaten egg to keep the dough from becoming soggy later.
3. Place the sliced peaches in a large bowl, and sprinkle with lemon juice. Mix gently. In a separate bowl, mix together the flour, sugar, cinnamon, nutmeg and salt. Pour over the peaches, and mix gently. Pour into the pie crust, and dot with butter. Cover with the other pie crust, and fold the edges under. Flute the edges to seal or press the edges with the tines of a fork dipped in egg. Brush the remaining egg over the top crust. Cut several slits in the top crust to vent steam.
4. Bake for 10 minutes in the preheated oven, then reduce the heat to 350 degrees F (175 degrees C) and bake for an additional 30 to 35 minutes, until the crust is brown and the juice begins to bubble through the vents. If the edges brown to fast, cover them with strips of aluminum foil about halfway through baking. Cool before serving. This tastes better warm than hot.

DARK CHOCOLATE CAKE

Servings: 12 | Prep: 20m | Cooks: 35m | Total: 55m

NUTRITION FACTS

Calories: 320 | Carbohydrates: 53.2g | Fat: 11.3g | Protein: 4.9g | Cholesterol: 33mg

INGREDIENTS

- 2 cups all-purpose flour
- 2 eggs
- 2 cups white sugar
- 1 cup cold brewed coffee
- 3/4 cup unsweetened cocoa
- 1 cup milk

- 2 teaspoons baking soda
- 1/2 cup vegetable oil
- 1 teaspoon baking powder
- 2 teaspoons vinegar
- 1/2 teaspoon salt

DIRECTIONS

1. Preheat oven to 350 degrees F (175 degrees C). Grease and flour a 9x13-inch pan.
2. In a large bowl, combine the flour, sugar, cocoa, baking soda, baking powder and salt. Make a well in the center and pour in the eggs, coffee, milk, oil and vinegar. Mix until smooth; the batter will be thin. Pour the batter into the prepared pan.
3. Bake in the preheated oven for 35 to 40 minutes, or until a toothpick inserted into the center of the cake comes out clean. Allow to cool.

OLD FASHIONED PEACH COBBLER
Servings: 18 | Prep: 30m | Cooks: 1h10m | Total: 2h10m

NUTRITION FACTS

Calories: 338 | Carbohydrates: 43.7g | Fat: 17.6g | Protein: 2.3g | Cholesterol: 26mg

INGREDIENTS

- 2 1/2 cups all-purpose flour
- 3/4 cup orange juice
- 3 tablespoons white sugar
- 1/2 cup butter
- 1 teaspoon salt
- 2 cups white sugar
- 1 cup shortening
- 1/2 teaspoon ground nutmeg
- 1 egg
- 1 teaspoon ground cinnamon
- 1/4 cup cold water
- 1 tablespoon cornstarch
- 3 pounds fresh peaches - peeled, pitted, and sliced
- 1 tablespoon white sugar
- 1/4 cup lemon juice
- 1 tablespoon butter, melted

DIRECTIONS

1. In a medium bowl, sift together the flour, 3 tablespoons sugar, and salt. Work in the shortening with a pastry blender until the mixture resembles coarse crumbs. In a small bowl, whisk together the egg and cold water. Sprinkle over flour mixture, and work with hands to form dough into a ball. Chill 30 minutes.
2. Preheat oven to 350 degrees F (175 degrees C). Roll out half of dough to 1/8 inch thickness. Place in a 9x13 inch baking dish, covering bottom and halfway up sides. Bake for 20 minutes, or until golden brown.
3. In a large saucepan, mix the peaches, lemon juice, and orange juice. Add 1/2 cup butter, and cook over medium-low heat until butter is melted. In a mixing bowl, stir together 2 cups sugar, nutmeg, cinnamon, and cornstarch; mix into peach mixture. Remove from heat, and pour into baked crust.
4. Roll remaining dough to a thickness of 1/4 inch. Cut into half-inch-wide strips. Weave strips into a lattice over peaches. Sprinkle with 1 tablespoon sugar, and drizzle with 1 tablespoon melted butter.
5. Bake in preheated oven for 35 to 40 minutes, or until top crust is golden brown.

BLUEBERRY COFFEE CAKE

Servings: 12 | Prep: 20m | Cooks: 1h | Total: 1h20m

NUTRITION FACTS

Calories: 401 | Carbohydrates: 61.1g | Fat: 16.3g | Protein: 4g | Cholesterol: 57mg

INGREDIENTS

- 1 cup packed brown sugar
- 1/2 cup butter
- 2/3 cup all-purpose flour
- 1 cup white sugar
- 1 teaspoon ground cinnamon
- 1 egg
- 1/2 cup butter
- 1 teaspoon vanilla extract
- 2 cups all-purpose flour
- 1/2 cup milk
- 2 teaspoons baking powder
- 1 cup fresh blueberries
- 1/2 teaspoon salt
- 1/4 cup confectioners' sugar for dusting

DIRECTIONS

1. Heat oven to 350 degrees F (175 degrees C). Coat a Bundt pan well with cooking spray.
2. Make the streusel topping: Mix 1 brown cup sugar, 2/3 cup flour, and cinnamon in a medium bowl. Cut in 1/2 cup butter or margarine; topping mixture will be crumbly. Set aside.

3. For the cake: Beat 1/2 cup butter or margarine in large bowl until creamy; add 1 cup white sugar, and beat until fluffy. Beat in egg and vanilla. Whisk together 2 cups flour, baking powder, and salt; add alternately with the milk to the creamed mixture, beating well after each addition.

4. Spread half the batter in the prepared pan. Cover with berries, and add remaining batter by tablespoons. Cover with streusel topping.

5. Bake at 350 degrees F (175 degrees C) for 55 to 60 minutes, until deep golden brown. Remove pan to wire rack to cool. Invert onto a plate after cake has cooled, and dust with confectioners' sugar.

CARROT PINEAPPLE CAKE
Servings: 24 | Prep: 30m | Cooks: 45m | Total: 1h15m

NUTRITION FACTS

Calories: 329 | Carbohydrates: 37.6g | Fat: 19.1g | Protein: 3.6g | Cholesterol: 39mg

INGREDIENTS

- 2 cups all-purpose flour
- 1 teaspoon vanilla extract
- 2 teaspoons baking soda
- 2 cups shredded carrots
- 1 teaspoon baking powder
- 1 cup flaked coconut
- 1 teaspoon salt
- 1 cup chopped walnuts
- 2 teaspoons ground cinnamon
- 1 (8 ounce) can crushed pineapple, drained
- 1 3/4 cups white sugar
- 1 (8 ounce) package cream cheese
- 1 cup vegetable oil
- 1/4 cup butter, softened
- 3 eggs
- 2 cups confectioners' sugar

DIRECTIONS

1. Preheat oven to 350 degrees F (175 degrees C). Grease and flour a 9x13 inch pan.

2. Mix flour, baking soda, baking powder, salt and cinnamon. Make a well in the center and add sugar, oil, eggs and vanilla. Mix with wooden spoon until smooth. Stir in carrots, coconut, walnuts and pineapple.

3. Pour into 9x13 inch pan. Bake at 350 degrees for about 45 minutes. Don't panic, the center will sink a little. Allow to cool.
4. To make the frosting: Cream the butter and cream cheese until smooth. Add the confectioners sugar and beat until creamy.

STRAWBERRY PRETZEL SALAD
Servings: 12 | Prep: 35m | Cooks: 10m | Total: 45m

NUTRITION FACTS

Calories: 424 | Carbohydrates: 52.1g | Fat: 23.3g | Protein: 4.5g | Cholesterol: 51mg

INGREDIENTS

- 2 cups crushed pretzels
- 1 (8 ounce) container frozen whipped topping, thawed
- 3/4 cup butter, melted
- 2 (3 ounce) packages strawberry flavored Jell-O
- 3 tablespoons white sugar
- 2 cups boiling water
- 1 (8 ounce) package cream cheese, softened
- 2 (10 ounce) packages frozen strawberries
- 1 cup white sugar

DIRECTIONS

1. Preheat oven to 400 degrees F (200 degrees C).
2. Stir together crushed pretzels, melted butter and 3 tablespoons sugar; mix well and press mixture into the bottom of a 9x13 inch baking dish.
3. Bake 8 to 10 minutes, until set. Set aside to cool.
4. In a large mixing bowl cream together cream cheese and 1 cup sugar. Fold in whipped topping. Spread mixture onto cooled crust.
5. Dissolve gelatin in boiling water. Stir in still frozen strawberries and allow to set briefly. When mixture is about the consistency of egg whites, pour and spread over cream cheese layer. Refrigerate until set.

EASY MINT CHOCOLATE CHIP ICE CREAM
Servings: 8 | Prep: 15m | Cooks: 2h | Total: 2h45m

NUTRITION FACTS

Calories: 439 | Carbohydrates: 43.2g | Fat: 29.7g | Protein: 4.1g | Cholesterol: 86mg

INGREDIENTS

- 2 cups 2% milk
- 1 teaspoon vanilla extract
- 2 cups heavy cream
- 1 teaspoon peppermint extract
- 1 cup sugar
- 3 drops green food coloring (optional)
- 1/2 teaspoon salt
- 1 cup miniature semisweet chocolate chips

DIRECTIONS

1. In a large bowl, stir together the milk, cream, sugar, salt, vanilla extract and peppermint extract until the sugar has dissolved. Color to your liking with the green food coloring.
2. Pour the mixture into an ice cream maker, and freeze according to the manufacturer's instructions. After about 10 minutes into the freezing, add the chocolate chips. After the ice cream has thickened, about 30 minutes later, spoon into a container, and freeze for 2 hours.

APPLE PIE

Servings: 8 | Prep: 20m | Cooks: 40m | Total: 1h

NUTRITION FACTS

Calories: 248 | Carbohydrates: 42.2g | Fat: 9.1g | Protein: 1.7g | Cholesterol: 4mg

INGREDIENTS

- 6 cups thinly sliced apples
- 1 teaspoon ground cinnamon
- 3/4 cup white sugar
- 1 recipe pastry for a 9-inch double-crust pie
- 1 tablespoon butter

DIRECTIONS

1. Prepare your pastry for a two crust pie. Wipe, quarter, core, peel, and slice apples; measure to 6 cups.
2. Combine sugar and cinnamon. The amount of sugar used depends on how tart your apples are.
3. Arrange apples in layers in pastry lined pie plate. Sprinkle each layer with sugar and cinnamon. Dot top layer with small pieces of butter or margarine. Cover with top crust.

4. Place on lowest rack in oven preheated to 450 degrees F (230 degrees C). Bake for 10 minutes, then reduce oven temperature to 350 degrees F (175 degrees C). Bake for 30 to 35 minutes longer. Serve warm or cold.

CHOCOLATE BOURBON PECAN PIE

Servings: 8 | Prep: 30m | Cooks: 1h | Total: 1h30m

NUTRITION FACTS

Calories: 647 | Carbohydrates: 79.9g | Fat: 35.4g | Protein: 6.1g | Cholesterol: 124mg

INGREDIENTS

- 1 (9 inch) pie shell
- 1/4 cup bourbon
- 1 cup white sugar
- 1 teaspoon vanilla extract
- 1 cup light corn syrup
- 1/4 teaspoon salt
- 1/2 cup butter
- 6 ounces semisweet chocolate chips
- 4 eggs, beaten
- 1 cup chopped pecans

DIRECTIONS

1. Preheat oven to 325 degrees F (165 degrees F).
2. In a small saucepan combine sugar, corn syrup, and butter or margarine. Cook over medium heat, stirring constantly, until butter or margarine melts and sugar dissolves. Cool slightly.
3. In a large bowl combine eggs, bourbon, vanilla, and salt. Mix well. Slowly pour sugar mixture into egg mixture, whisking constantly. Stir in chocolate chips and pecans. Pour mixture into pie shell.
4. Bake in preheated oven for 50 to 55 minutes, or until set and golden. May be served warm or chilled.

POUND CAKE

Servings: 30 | Prep: 30m | Cooks: 1h10m | Total: 1h40m

NUTRITION FACTS

Calories: 264 | Carbohydrates: 33.1g | Fat: 13.5g | Protein: 3.3g | Cholesterol: 70mg

INGREDIENTS

- 2 cups butter
- 4 cups all-purpose flour
- 3 cups white sugar
- 2/3 cup milk
- 6 eggs

DIRECTIONS

1. Preheat oven to 350 degrees F (175 degrees C). Grease 3 - 8x4 inch loaf pans, then line with parchment paper.
2. In a large bowl, cream together the butter and sugar until light and fluffy. Beat in the eggs one at a time. Beat in the flour alternately with the milk, mixing just until incorporated.
3. Pour batter evenly into prepared loaf pans. Bake in the preheated oven for 70 minutes, or until a toothpick inserted into the center of the cakes comes out clean. After removing them from the oven, immediately loosen cake edges with a knife. Allow to cool in pans for 10 minutes, then remove from the pans. Strip off the parchment paper and cool completely on wire racks.

BUTTERSCOTCH BREAD PUDDING

Servings: 8 | Prep: 10m | Cooks: 1h | Total: 1h10m

NUTRITION FACTS

Calories: 623 | Carbohydrates: 92.6g | Fat: 23.1g | Protein: 9.4g | Cholesterol: 110mg

INGREDIENTS

- 1 (10.75 ounce) loaf day-old bread, torn into small pieces
- 3 eggs, beaten
- 4 cups milk
- 2 teaspoons vanilla extract
- 2 cups brown sugar
- 1 cup butterscotch chips
- 1/2 cup butter, melted

DIRECTIONS

1. Preheat oven to 350 degrees F (175 degrees C). Butter a 9x13 inch baking dish.
2. In a large bowl, combine bread, milk, sugar, butter, eggs, vanilla and butterscotch chips; mixture should be the consistency of oatmeal. Pour into prepared pan.
3. Bake in preheated oven 1 hour, until nearly set. (It should have a "thigh wiggle" or wiggle as much as a well endowed thigh.) Serve warm or cold.

APPLE BREAD PUDDING

Servings: 8 | Prep: 15m | Cooks: 45m | Total: 1h

NUTRITION FACTS

Calories: 430 | Carbohydrates: 58.8g | Fat: 20g | Protein: 5.6g | Cholesterol: 52mg

INGREDIENTS

- 4 cups soft bread cubes
- 1/2 teaspoon vanilla extract
- 1/4 cup raisins
- 2 eggs, beaten
- 2 cups peeled and sliced apples
- 1/4 cup white sugar
- 1 cup brown sugar
- 1/4 cup brown sugar
- 1 3/4 cups milk
- 1/2 cup milk
- 1/4 cup margarine
- 1/2 cup margarine
- 1 teaspoon ground cinnamon
- 1 teaspoon vanilla extract

DIRECTIONS

1. Preheat oven to 350 degrees F (175 degrees C). Grease a 7x11 inch baking dish.
2. In a large bowl, combine bread, raisins, and apples. In a small saucepan over medium heat, combine 1 cup brown sugar, 1 3/4 cups milk, and 1/4 cup margarine. Cook and stir until margarine is melted. Pour over bread mixture in bowl.
3. In a small bowl, whisk together cinnamon, 1/2 teaspoon vanilla, and eggs. Pour bread mixture into prepared dish, and pour egg mixture over bread.
4. Bake in preheated oven 40 to 50 minutes, or until center is set and apples are tender.
5. While pudding is baking, mix together sugar, 1/4 cup brown sugar, 1/2 cup milk, and 1/2 cup margarine in a saucepan. Bring to a boil, then remove from heat, and stir in 1 teaspoon vanilla. Serve over bread pudding.

APPLE DUMPLINGS

Servings: 8 | Prep: 20m | Cooks: 35m | Total: 55m

NUTRITION FACTS

Calories: 416 | Carbohydrates: 58.2g | Fat: 19.3g | Protein: 4g | Cholesterol: 31mg

INGREDIENTS

- 1 (16 ounce) can refrigerated flaky biscuit dough
- 1/2 cup butter, melted
- 4 apples - peeled, cored and halved
- 2 teaspoons vanilla extract
- 1 cup white sugar
- 1/2 teaspoon ground cinnamon
- 1 cup water

DIRECTIONS

1. Preheat oven to 350 degrees F (175 degrees C).
2. Butter a 7x11 inch baking pan. Separate biscuit dough into 8 pieces. Flatten each piece of dough into a circle. Wrap one biscuit around each apple half and place, seam side down, in pan.
3. In small bowl, combine sugar, water, melted butter and vanilla. Pour mixture over dumplings in pan. Sprinkle cinnamon on top. Bake 35 to 40 minutes, until golden. Serve hot.

OATMEAL BUTTERSCOTCH COOKIES
Servings: 48 | Prep: 15m | Cooks: 10m | Total: 25m

NUTRITION FACTS

Calories: 119 | Carbohydrates: 16.2g | Fat: 5.1g | Protein: 1.3g | Cholesterol: 15mg

INGREDIENTS

- 3/4 cup butter, softened
- 1 teaspoon baking soda
- 3/4 cup white sugar
- 1/2 teaspoon ground cinnamon
- 3/4 cup packed brown sugar
- 1/2 teaspoon salt
- 2 eggs
- 3 cups rolled oats
- 1 teaspoon vanilla extract
- 1 2/3 cups butterscotch chips
- 1 1/4 cups all-purpose flour

DIRECTIONS

1. Preheat oven to 375 degrees F (190 degrees C).
2. In a large bowl beat the butter or margarine, white sugar and brown sugar together. Add the eggs and vanilla, beating well.

3. Stir together the flour, baking soda, cinnamon and salt. Gradually add the flour mixture to the butter mixture and stir until blended. Stir in the oats and the butterscotch chips. Drop by teaspoonfuls onto an ungreased cookie sheet.
4. Bake for 8 to 10 minutes in the preheated oven, until the edges begin to brown.

WHIPPED SHORTBREAD COOKIES

Servings: 36 | Prep: 15m | Cooks: 20m | Total: 35m

NUTRITION FACTS

Calories: 75 | Carbohydrates: 6.8g | Fat: 5.2g | Protein: 0.6g | Cholesterol: 14mg

INGREDIENTS

- 1 cup butter, softened
- 1/4 cup red maraschino cherries, quartered
- 1 1/2 cups all-purpose flour
- 1/4 cup green maraschino cherries, quartered
- 1/2 cup confectioners' sugar

DIRECTIONS

1. Preheat oven to 350 degrees F (175 degrees C).
2. In a large bowl, combine butter, flour, and confectioners' sugar. With an electric mixer, beat for 10 minutes, until light and fluffy. Spoon onto cookie sheets, spacing cookies 2 inches apart. Place a piece of maraschino cherry onto the middle of each cookie, alternating between red and green.
3. Bake for 15 to 17 minutes in the preheated oven, or until the bottoms of the cookies are lightly browned. Remove from oven, and let cool on cookie sheet for 5 minutes, then transfer cookies on to wire rack to cool. Store in an airtight container, separating each layer with waxed paper.

My Sight Word List

English - Italian

a	in	said
and	is	see
away	it	the
big	jump	three
blue	little	to
can	look	two
come	make	up
down	me	we
find	my	where
for	not	yellow
funny	one	you
go	day	
help	play	
here	red	
I	run	

Name: ______________________ Date: ______________________

Today is: Monday Tuesday Wednesday Thursday Friday

Direction: Trace and read the sentences.

fun	gun	run	sun
	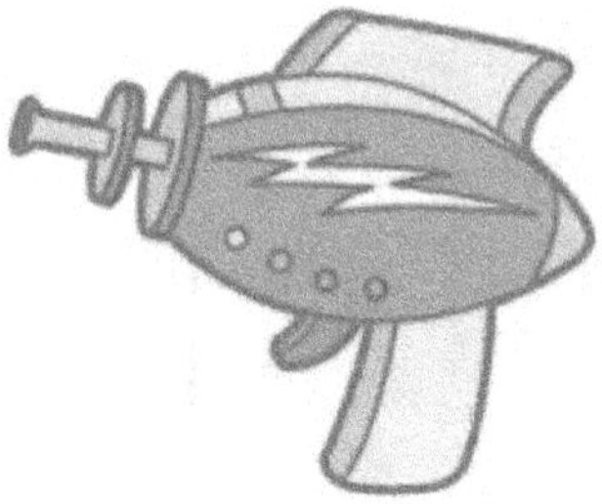		
godere	pistola	correre	sole

 They are having fun.

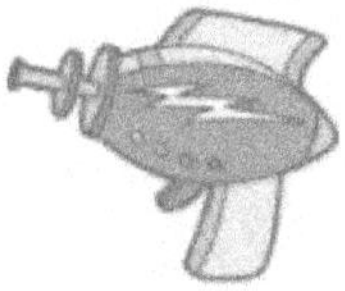 He has a gun.

 The bear is running.

 The sun is smiling.